CHRISTIAN ENCOUNTERS

GEORGE WASHINGTON CARVER

CHRISTIAN ENCOUNTERS SERIES

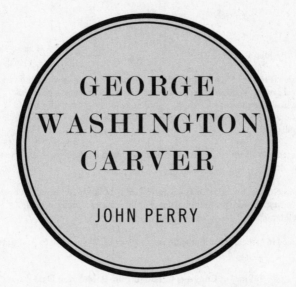

GEORGE WASHINGTON CARVER

JOHN PERRY

Thomas Nelson

Since 1798

NASHVILLE   DALLAS   MEXICO CITY   RIO DE JANEIRO

Published in Nashville, Tennessee. Thomas Nelson is a trademark of Thomas Nelson, Inc.

Thomas Nelson, Inc., titles may be purchased in bulk for educational, business, fund-raising, or sales promotional use. For information, please e-mail SpecialMarkets@ThomasNelson.com.

Published in association with the literary agency of Wolgemuth & Associates, Inc.

Library of Congress Cataloging-in-Publication Data

Perry, John, 1952-
  George Washington Carver / John Perry.
    p. cm. -- (Christian encounters series)
  Includes bibliographical references.
  ISBN 978-1-59555-026-2
1. Carver, George Washington, 1864?-1943. 2. African American
agriculturists--Biography. 3. Agriculturists--United States--Biography. I. Title.
S417.C3P37 2011
  630.92--dc22
  [B]

                            2011006173

              Printed in the United States of America

            11 12 13 14 15 HCI 6 5 4 3 2 1

To my brother, Scott,
whose kindness and gentleness
are part of what makes him
such an inspiring husband,
father, brother, and friend.

CONTENTS

1

CARVER'S GEORGE

Southwestern Missouri in the winter of 1863 was a lawless and deadly land. The war that ripped the United States in two had divided Missouri families against themselves. Though a slaveholding state, the legislature had voted in 1861 to stand with the Union even as Confederate sympathies ran strong. Governor Claiborne Jackson himself led an army of secessionist irregulars on one bloody raid after another. The southwest corner of the state in particular endured endless skirmishes as the two sides fought for control. Making a bad situation worse, the region was a crossroads for soldiers, militiamen, marauders, scavengers, opportunists, bounty hunters, and deserters traveling between the Union and the Confederacy, some with shifting loyalties, others who willingly took the law into their own hands. From rebel Arkansas to the south, raiders came to capture escaped slaves and return them for a reward. Abolitionists rode in from Kansas to the west, once a slave-holding territory and now a free state with its own bloody history, to help Missouri defend itself against homegrown adversaries. In between Arkansas and Kansas, the Oklahoma Indian Territory offered vast empty spaces to hide vigilante patrols, recruit soldiers for both sides, and for runaway slaves to disappear into the trackless plains.

Marion Township, just outside Diamond Grove near the Newton County seat of Neosho, was a rural settlement in the thickest of the Missouri guerrilla fighting. Confederates took over the county government and adopted an ordinance of secession, though in Neosho the Union loyalists likely outnumbered Southern sympathizers. Raiders and looters galloped through the countryside day and night, as did ordinary criminals who found opportunity in the confusion and lawlessness of the moment.

One of the five slaveholders listed in the Marion Township census of 1860 was Moses Carver. He and his wife, Susan, were relatively prosperous farmers, though they lived modestly and seemed to have no material wealth beyond what their neighbors did. Carver was also a successful stock trader and horse trainer. The couple had no children, which was a liability because farmers needed children to keep a place in good order; tending crops, cultivating a kitchen garden, caring for livestock, repairing fences and gates, cutting firewood, drawing water, and maintaining equipment was more than a couple alone could do. Like many Americans before him, Moses Carver was against the idea of one human being owning another but saw slavery as an economic necessity. The 1860 census listed Carver as owning two slaves, a woman named Mary and her mulatto (half white) infant son, Jim, born the previous October. Carver had bought Mary for seven hundred dollars in 1855 when she was thirteen. A female slave's children became the property of her owner.

By late 1863 Mary had another son, George. As with most children born in the countryside, especially slaves, there was no record of his birth. In later years George said he had been born in 1864 or '65. It is possible that a baby recorded as born in Marion Township on July 12, 1860, was George. A birth date so soon after his brother's indicated he arrived prematurely. That would account for his being small, frail, and hampered by severe breathing problems—conditions associated with premature birth, and which he dealt with all his life. George never knew his father, who died either before he was born or about that time. Again no official accounts exist, though in describing his early years, George wrote in 1922 that his father was the property of Mr. Grant, owner of the plantation next door, and was killed soon after George was born "while hauling wood with an ox team. In some way he fell from the load, under the wagon, both wheels passing over him."[1]

Mary and her boys lived in what had once been Moses and Susan's cabin, a one-room log building with a fireplace, one window opening with shutters but no glass (a rare and expensive luxury on the frontier), and a packed earth floor. Earlier the Carvers had shared it with Moses' brother's three children, two boys and a girl, whom they raised after their father died. The children were grown and gone by 1860, and at some point the Carvers built a similar but larger home for themselves and gave their old home to Mary and her boys.

Some slaveholders in southwestern Missouri abandoned their homesteads during the war in the face of threats, raids, and destruction, but Moses would not be frightened off his property. After decades of work, he had built one of the most valuable farms in town, with a hundred acres under cultivation, an orchard, beehives, and a range of livestock. Though others might buckle under the pressure, Moses Carver was a stubborn man when he believed he was right.

Stories vary as to how many times the Carver farm was raided. There is one account that robbers came demanding money, which Carver refused. They ordered him to reveal where his savings were hidden. When he still said nothing, they hung him by his thumbs and burned his feet with hot coals. Stubborn Moses remained silent until the raiders finally gave up.

Either then or during another raid, invaders made off with property far more valuable to the Carvers than buried cash. One bitter cold November day Moses was working in the field and had Jim with him, while Mary was in her cabin with George. Seeing the attackers ride up, Moses and Jim hid from them, but Mary and George were kidnapped.

The men may have been traders or bounty hunters planning to sell captured slaves in Arkansas. As soon as they left, Moses started planning to rescue Mary and her boy, but he had no idea where to look first. His neighbor, Sergeant John Bentley, was a Union scout who knew the shadowy world of bushwhackers and vigilantes in the region and agreed to help. Moses promised a racehorse and forty acres of land for the return of his property. Riding through the night, Sergeant Bentley and his search party found George alone in an abandoned cabin. Bentley instructed the others to continue the chase, then carried the boy home and laid him in the crib with his own son for the night. The next day Bentley returned George to the Carvers and reported there was no sign of Mary. George's mother was never heard from again. Since the sergeant had found one slave but not the other, Moses gave him part of the reward: a fine horse valued at three hundred dollars.

Susan and Moses moved the two motherless slave boys into their house to raise as their own. Technically they remained slaves until a new state constitution was enacted on July 4, 1865, since the Emancipation Proclamation covered only the Confederacy. Yet practically, from the time Mary disappeared, the Carvers loved and cared for George and Jim as blood kin, just as they had cared for their niece and nephews years before. The brothers even assumed the Carver family name.

After the end of the war, the newly constituted Carver family settled down to life on the farm. Jim grew tall and strong and, like a typical farm boy, took on a list of chores at an early age. By his teens he could handle a day's work equal to what a man could do. His younger brother was a different story entirely. George remained a slight, sickly boy who fought off one respiratory illness after another. His constant coughing and breathing problems could have been symptoms of bronchitis, pneumonia, or even tuberculosis. His adoptive parents diagnosed whooping cough or croup. Whatever the cause, he coughed and hacked so much that he sometimes lost his voice.

Clearly George would never be able to shoulder his share

of the farmwork a boy was expected to do. So instead of learning to plow, build a fence, and repair a piece of machinery, he learned to take care of the kitchen garden, gather eggs, and help Susan with the cooking, laundry, and other housework. Then or later he also learned to sew and crochet.

Moses Carver was known in the community as a man who understood animals. He raised and traded horses, mules, hogs, and other livestock, and had a pet rooster trained to perch on his shoulder. Added to his experience with crops, fruit trees, and bees, his animal knowledge made Moses something of an expert on the natural world in general. As George grew older, he became attracted to nature as well. He spent hours in the orchard and in the vegetable garden near the house. He planted a flower garden of his own; though he kept it a secret because he thought his foster parents would consider it a waste of time. George had what later generations would call a green thumb. Even the neighbors started noticing how attentive he was to plants, how he could make things grow, and especially how he could coax sick plants back to health.

Every moment he wasn't busy with housework George spent in the gardens or in the woods. He started collecting plant samples and rocks, along with frogs and other small animals he could slip in his pockets. Happy as Susan was to see George's fascination with nature, after one surprise too many she started making him turn his pockets out before he came inside. She also convinced him to pare down his rock collection after he piled them so high beside the hearth that she feared the whole stack would collapse.

George loved learning and was as eager to go to school as he was to know about plants. The Locust Grove School was only a mile or so away, but it didn't allow black children to attend. The same building hosted church services on Sunday and Wednesday, along with occasional shows by traveling comedy troupes. George was welcome at Locust Grove then, even though he couldn't attend school within the same four walls on the other days. The Carvers didn't go to church, but George was so interested in Christianity that he walked the mile by himself every Sunday morning. His Sunday school teacher, Flora Abbott, gave young George special encouragement. She recognized his passion for learning, helping him memorize Bible verses and assuring him that "the Lord heard and answered the prayers of a child just as surely as He did that of their parents."[2] Mrs. Abbott also nurtured George's love for music. He started singing in church at Locust Grove and learned to pick out melodies on the piano. Music had been part of George's life for as long as he could remember. Moses Carver played the fiddle so well that he was in constant demand at dances and picnics.

George Carver developed into a shy older boy. Because he was physically weak he didn't play with the others, preferring to stay on the sidelines and watch, even though sometimes other boys teased him for not joining in. He was consumed with the desire to know more about everything, and his playmates teased him about that too. Quiet and set apart as he was, he still had plenty of friends among the Carver relatives and neighbors. Black and white children played together as equals; only later were they taught that one race was inferior to the other.

Susan Carver did her best to satisfy George's hunger for knowledge by teaching him herself from a copy of Noah Webster's *Elementary Spelling Book*, known universally as the "blue-backed speller," one of the most widely used textbooks in America. Combining Susan's teaching with Mrs. Abbott's Sunday lessons, George learned to read and write, always longing to know more. On his walks he began praying for a chance to learn more about the plants he so enjoyed, and that God would direct his life.

The blue-backed speller couldn't begin to answer all the questions swirling around inside George's head. When an educated black man moved to Diamond Grove, Moses hired him to tutor George. It wasn't long though before George's curiosity took him beyond the tutor's abilities. Finally, Moses found a school in Neosho that would take "colored" students. George moved to the county seat, boarding with a couple named Andrew and Mariah Watkins. It was the first time he could remember living in a household headed by black people.

Mariah was a laundress. Since George had learned to do laundry at the Carvers, he eagerly pitched in to help Mariah with her work. She was also a midwife with a wealth of knowledge about the medicinal uses for plants. George absorbed everything she would tell him about them and still begged for more. Mariah was a devout Christian who took George to church and encouraged him to read the Bible. She told him about the slave named Libby who had taught her to read. "You must learn all you can, then be like Libby," she said. "Go out in the world and give your learning back to our people."[3] That Christmas

Mariah Watkins gave George a Bible, which he kept for the rest of his life.

Until he moved to Neosho, George had not used a last name. As a slave, he may have been referred to as "Carver's George." Mrs. Watkins thought a student ought to have a last name, and so enrolled him as George Carver. The teacher was a young black man named Stephen Frost, known to the students as "the professor." Like so many black educators in the Reconstruction period after the Civil War, he was poorly trained, poorly paid, and ill equipped for his work. As he had outpaced his tutor in Diamond Grove, George soon knew everything Professor Frost did. When George solved a math problem and the professor insisted he was wrong, George took the answer to a white teacher in town and got her to sign it saying it was correct.

Within a year or so George Carver had learned all that the school in Neosho could teach. He received his graduation certificate on December 22, 1876, and immediately began looking for a way to continue his education. When he heard that a family from Neosho was traveling to Fort Scott, Kansas, where there was a school open to blacks and whites alike, he convinced them to take him along. Within a few days, George bid the Watkins goodbye, collected his Bible and a few clothes, and headed west, walking most of the seventy-five miles because the wagon was too full of furniture to ride. They were headed for what widely distributed handbills called "Sunny Kansas," where emancipated slaves were streaming for the offer of free land and a fresh start.

WANDERING YEARS

The first order of business for young George in Fort Scott was to find a job and a place to live. He came to town literally penniless, and so would have to work and save money before he could start school. What George lacked in physical strength he made up for in dedication and enthusiasm. Felix Payne and his wife were looking for a hired girl to cook and do housework. Carver applied for the job and Payne, a blacksmith, decided to give the teenager a chance. Growing up helping Susan Carver around the house, George learned to cook and serve meals, wash clothes, and do other chores. He tackled his new responsibilities enthusiastically. Every dish washed, every shirt ironed brought him closer to starting classes. He also worked part time at a grocery store across the street from the Paynes, and took in laundry for guests of the Wilder House hotel.

The moment he could afford it, George enrolled in school. When the money ran out, he quit long enough to earn another small stake, then picked up where he left off. He was an excellent student despite his erratic attendance. Carver spent two happy years in Fort Scott. At last he had the chance to get the education he had wanted for so long, and under normal circumstances he might have settled in town indefinitely.

But Carver's future was redirected on the night of March 26, 1879, when a black man was accused of raping a twelve-year-old white girl and thrown in the county jail. Wearing masks, a mob of thirty men swarmed the jail, grabbed the suspect, and hanged him from a lamppost as a huge crowd watched. Then they dragged the body through the streets, stopping in front of the Payne house to beat his brains out on the curb as George watched in terror from his window. Later the corpse was doused with kerosene and set on fire. Though he had seen and experienced discrimination all his life, George had lived mostly with white families who treated him as an equal. A savage lynching before a cheering crowd of a thousand or more was unimaginable to him. "As young as I was," Carver remembered a lifetime later, "the horror haunted me and does even now."[1]

Carver left Fort Scott immediately, moving to a school in Paola, Kansas, which, although segregated, did accept black students. There he discovered that his on-again-off-again education to date had taken him only partway through elementary school. In his mid-to late teens by now, George was a head taller than his younger classmates despite being small for his age. Before long he got a job as housekeeper for Ben and Lucy Seymour in the town of Olathe. Though the Seymours were black, their two nieces, Sally and Geneva Cross, were allowed to attend the school in Olathe, and George started going with them. To help pay his expenses, he also helped Lucy with her work as a laundress and did odd jobs for the Cross girls' father, a barber.

Mariah Watkins had planted seeds of Christianity in George while he lived with her family in Neosho, taking him every week to the African Methodist Episcopal Church. In Olathe he attended the Methodist church and started teaching Sunday school. His early fascination with nature paved the way for him to love and worship the Creator of all things. Around this time he also reaffirmed his interest in music by learning to play the accordion. Often at the end of the day he sat in the window of his room and played for people walking by.

Sometime in mid-1880, the Seymours moved west to Minneapolis, Kansas, and George followed shortly afterward. By the end of the year, Carver had borrowed a little more than two hundred fifty dollars to open George Carver's Laundry in an empty shack in a run-down part of town known as Poverty Gulch. To the townspeople's amazement, he soon had the dilapidated place up and running, improving the look of an old neighborhood eyesore in the process.

George picked up his loads at the general store, carrying them down to the gulch in a basket on his back, then made the return trip up with stacks of clothes freshly washed, ironed, and folded. That such immaculate-looking wash could come out of what had been such a pit of a place impressed everyone who saw it. On his way in and out of the store George admired a big vase that was always full of fresh flowers. One day he asked the owner if he could buy the vase for a small down payment and the rest in washing. The owner thought Carver was crazy to take anything beautiful into Poverty Gulch, but agreed to it anyway.

George enrolled in the integrated Minneapolis public school as an eighth grader. Although he was nearly twenty, he was about the same size as the other boys and looked more or less their age. Adding to the impression that he was younger than he was, his voice had never changed, probably because of all the serious childhood illnesses. (He kept a boy's voice all his life; people hearing him speak for the first time were often startled at the sound.) George once again was an excellent student, earning high marks even as he divided his time running his laundry and doing odd jobs for Dr. James McHenry. Lucy Seymour worked as a nurse for McHenry; George drove the doctor on his rounds, carried his medical bag, and took care of his horses.

During the two years Carver attended school in Minneapolis, he built his laundry service to the point where he could invest in two lots in town, buying them for a hundred dollars and selling them ten months later for five hundred. On July 29, 1883, he joined the racially integrated Presbyterian church where the Seymours were members, and where one of his best friends was a white boy named Chester Rarig. Once again it seemed that Carver might settle down for good, staying in Minneapolis, finishing high school, and continuing with his successful business.

Instead, Carver changed course and decided to pursue a professional career. With his real estate profits he moved east to

Kansas City and enrolled in business school. His friend Chester was with him at least part of the time, which led to awkward moments when a lunch counter would serve Chester but not George. Applying himself with his usual dedication, Carver quickly mastered typing and shorthand and found a job as a stenographer at the telegraph office in the railroad terminal.

Against all odds, George Carver now had a marketable skill, a steady job, and money in the bank. Yet for all his accomplishments, he couldn't rest because he couldn't shake his longing for a higher education. For so many years he had struggled to advance his learning because he had no regular income. Now that he had the means, he couldn't bear not to continue learning.

Carver applied for admission to Highland College, a Presbyterian school north of Kansas City in the northeast corner of the state. The day he received his acceptance letter was one of the happiest of his young life. It wasn't far from Kansas City to Highland, but George decided to take time to visit old friends before he settled down at college. He traveled west by rail on a half-fare ticket, with the conductor noting he was an awfully young boy to be traveling by himself. He went to see Moses and Susan Carver in Diamond Grove, where all the neighbors and church members welcomed him back, marveling at his accordion and even more so at his typewriter, a machine no one there had ever seen. Visitors brought slips of paper for George to type their names or a short message as a souvenir.

One of the neighbors invited him to bring his accordion to a hymn sing at his home, where a crowd gathered for music,

Bible reading, and prayer. In closing, the neighbor, Bedford Brown, shook Carver's hand and said, "George, you can go out into the world, and you may make a lot of money. Someone could sneak it from you. You get a good education and no one can ever take it from you."[2]

Brimming with anticipation, George Carver took the train to Highland and went straight to the president's office to get his class assignments. Reverend Brown, the college president, looked him up and down with an expression of surprise. "You didn't tell me you were a Negro. Highland College does not take Negroes."[3]

At first stunned, then devastated, Carver silently turned around and left the room. After so long a journey during his young life, from Marion Township and Diamond Grove to Neosho, Fort Scott, Paola, Olathe, Minneapolis, and Kansas City, he had expected to enroll at last in a real college. The disappointment must have been as deeply heartrending as his acceptance letter had been exhilarating.

Though he didn't tell anyone what had happened, word got around in the small rural community. Members of the church in Highland—black and white alike—reached out to him, inviting him to their homes. Before long they came to appreciate his skill at conversation and storytelling, and his ability on the accordion. He often played for his hosts after a meal. Carver resumed his familiar role as housekeeper for John Beeler, who owned an apple orchard south of town. Stepping into the Beeler kitchen for the first time, George learned that he faced two challenges: one, Mr. Beeler was a finicky eater; and two, he had not a single tooth in his head. George's solution was cornbread: hot, tasty, filling, and easy to gum. As John's daughter, Della, watched, her father took a small trial taste, then tucked into his serving ravenously, signaling for another piece and another until the whole skillet was empty.

Carver spent a year or so working for the Beelers, playing his accordion in the evenings after his work was done, and still studying plants on his own, gathering interesting specimens on his walks and marveling at how beautiful and varied God's creation was. As the shock and disappointment of his rejection at Highland faded, George began looking for other adventures and opportunities.

The Homestead Act of 1862 was to encourage settlers to move to western Kansas. Anyone willing to live there five years got a hundred and sixty acres of land for only a twenty-four-dollar filing fee, paid at the end of the five years. Mr. Beeler's son Frank headed west to try his hand at homesteading and opened a store in Ness County. A small settlement grew up around the store and became the tiny town of Beeler. In the summer of 1886, George followed Frank Beeler to Ness County. The *Ness County News* for the week of August 14 reported Carver's arrival, describing him by mistake as a student at Highland.

George found work as housekeeper for county commissioner George Steeley, a white resident of Eden Township. Like other homes in the treeless plains, Steeley's house was made of sod bricks with a tar-paper roof, though he did have the unusual luxury of a glass window, which had come seventy-five miles by train from the town of Larned. George quickly proved his worth in his employer's kitchen and laundry, and all went well until Steeley's mother came for a visit. She opposed Negroes spending time in the house, and especially eating with the family. As long as she stayed, George kept his distance and ate alone after the Steeleys had finished.

Carver staked his homestead claim and kept working and living at the Steeley house until he finished his own sod hut, fourteen feet square, with one opening for a window and another for a door. Since there were no trees for firewood, his cookstove ran on sunflower stalks and dried dung. When he moved in on April 18, 1887, he made room among his simple furniture for his washboard, washtub, flatirons, and accordion. George planted seventeen acres of crops and three dozen fruit trees using tools borrowed from Commissioner Steeley. He also bought ten chickens.

Until his first crop came in, Carver continued housekeeping for the commissioner, sleeping in his own hut at night to preserve his homestead claim. He made friends with his neighbors, who were impressed with his articulate speaking and musical skill. George was a likable young man and had an obvious gift for growing things, which was an especially valuable skill in so arid and barren a place. He was also earning a reputation as a painter of plants as well as an expert at growing them. With Steeley's permission he built a small addition onto the side of the Steeley hut and filled it with horticultural samples. George and his employer both enjoyed taking visitors into this "greenhouse" to see plants that appeared healthier and more lush than anyone could recall elsewhere in the county.

Life was harsh on the plains of western Kansas. Carver never dug a successful well on his property, and hauled water three-quarters of a mile from the Steeley place as long as he lived there. A winter blizzard raged so hard that he literally couldn't see his hand in front of his face. In spite of the harsh conditions, the hearty "soddies" held on. The *Ness City Times* of December 15, 1887, reported Carver's election as assistant editor of the literary society, referring to him as "Geo. W. Carver," possibly the first time any indication of a middle name appeared in print. George may have added it to differentiate himself from another George Carver in town. When someone asked him what the "W" stood for, he said, "Washington." Whatever the circumstances or inspiration, George chose his own middle name.

George was in the news again the next spring, when he caught a reporter's attention as a witness for another black man filing a homestead claim with the district court clerk. The more the reporter learned about this well-spoken young man, the more convinced he became that Carver was "by reason of his color and opportunity a somewhat remarkable character." The *Ness County News* for March 31, 1888, published a flattering portrait of Carver beginning with his birth as a slave, his early education, and his thwarted attempt at enrolling in college ("which one we are not informed"). The article went on:

> Failing in this he improved every opportunity for private study, which extended to many of the sciences. His

knowledge of geology, botany, and kindred sciences is remarkable, and makes him a man of more than ordinary ability.

He has a fair knowledge of painting, and some of his sketches have considerable merit. He came to Ness County a year and a half ago . . . When not employed on another tract which he has entered [as his homestead claim], he works for Mr. George Steeley, who, being a gentleman of high culture himself, takes great pleasure in encouraging his employee's literary and scientific inclinations. Carver has gathered a collection of about five hundred plants in a neat conservatory adjoining the residence of his employer, besides having a large geological collection in and around the place. He is a pleasant and intelligent man to talk with, and were it not for his dusky skin—no fault of his—he might occupy a different sphere to which his ability would otherwise entitle him.[4]

This rare early account is remarkably consistent with descriptions of Carver written decades later: a well-spoken intellectual, hard-working, dedicated both to art and to science, a tireless collector ever eager to know more about the natural world around him, a figure who but for his "dusky skin" would rise even higher in the world's esteem.

Like other homesteaders, Carver spent most of his time during the growing season working in the field. When winter blizzards and cold temperatures kept him inside, he played the accordion, crocheted lace, wrote poetry on his typewriter, and spent hours drawing and painting. He also took art lessons from

Clara Duncan, a homesteader who had taught art at Talladega College, one of the first colleges for blacks in America.

George would have owned his hundred and sixty acres if he'd lived there five years. However, by the summer of 1888 he had had enough of the frontier. He mortgaged his homestead for three hundred dollars and moved east, landing at last in Winterset, Iowa, where he found work as a hotel cook. He attended the Baptist church there, which, though not segregated, had only a handful of black people in the congregation. As before, he naturally gravitated toward white groups because he had lived so much of his life surrounded by whites. He sat quietly in the back row on Sundays, but his clear treble voice soon attracted attention. Dr. John Milholland looked George up at the hotel and said his wife wanted to meet him because she had heard his beautiful singing voice in church. The Milhollands invited George over for music and conversation, and before long he was stopping by their house every afternoon on his way home from work.

In a year George saved enough money to open a laundry in Winterset with plans to start school again. The Milhollands suggested he go to Simpson College a few miles away in Indianola. Still stung by his rejection at Highland, he applied anyway at their encouragement and was surprised and delighted when he was accepted. Since he didn't have a high school diploma, he began with the preparatory courses. He also took music lessons, which he paid for in paintings. When he started the semester on September 9, 1890, he was the only black student on campus. Rather than rejecting him, students were fascinated by him and impressed as well by his obvious intelligence and interest in so many things. However, George was still keenly aware of social nuances and, for example, would cross the street so a white girl who knew him wouldn't have to speak to him while she was walking with friends.

Carver had fifteen cents left over after paying his tuition. He spent ten cents on cornmeal and five on beef suet, then started canvassing his fellow students for laundry work. One of his new friends, John Morley, learned that Carver was living in a shack for free and had only boxes for furniture, along with a cookstove salvaged from the dump and a washtub and other laundry equipment bought on credit. He and others hired George to do their wash, bought him some furniture, and made some more out of scrap lumber. Knowing he wouldn't accept cash handouts, they slipped money or concert tickets under his door once in a while.

Simpson College must have seemed a taste of heaven on earth to George Carver. He was excelling at a "real" college, making friends, singing, painting, and throwing himself into church services and revivals. At the end of the school year he wrote to the Milhollands, "I remain your humble servant of God. I am learning to trust and realize the blessed result from trusting Him every day . . . I realize that God has a great work for me to do." He also displayed his talent for embellishing the truth, which remained a part of his personality all his life: "I can now sing up to high D and 8 octaves below. I have only had one lesson."[5] Eight octaves is more than the range of the entire piano keyboard.

George's art teacher at Simpson was one of the most important figures in his life. Etta Budd recognized Carver's incredible natural skill as a painter, and sensed that it stemmed from a genuine love of plants and all of nature. Yet she was afraid that no matter how good his paintings were, people would not buy works from a black artist. Miss Budd encouraged George, therefore, to study plants instead of painting them. Her father was a professor of agriculture at Iowa State College in Ames. When she left Simpson at the end of the school year to care for her mother at home, she told George he should come to Iowa State and turn his attention to science.

After thinking it over, George decided to take her advice. He knew his love of art and music would not fade. To that he would now add scientific training that would reveal the deepest mysteries of God's wonderful world.

THE ROAD TO TUSKEGEE

George Carver was the only black student at Iowa State in the fall of 1891. As such, he had to pick his way along an uneasy trail of social and practical challenges. Fortunately he found a staunch ally in Professor James Wilson, newly arrived on campus as director of the agricultural experiment station, who quickly recognized Carver's intellect and his natural skill and interest in horticulture.

The first hurdle was assigning him a dormitory room. Though no one spoke it aloud, the question on everyone's mind was, "Who's going to sleep with the colored boy?" Professor Wilson came to the rescue by giving George his office as living quarters. Later Carver lived in a single room in faculty housing. At the beginning of the year, the dining hall manager made George eat in the basement with the janitors, though George soon won him over and ate with the rest of his classmates from then on. Students and faculty alike quickly came to appreciate and befriend this earnest, hard-working black man. He took odd jobs around campus, including maintenance of the green-house and science labs. He made his own clothes and stretched his meager food budget by foraging for edible plants. A sympathetic dining hall cook supplied him with banquet leftovers. When other students realized he wasn't taking notes in class because he couldn't afford writing materials, they saved their pencil stubs for him.

George wrote to the Milhollands that he didn't like Iowa State at first. He was "anxious to be getting out and doing something" and felt that God was preparing him for a special purpose.

> The more my ideas develop, the more beautiful and grand seems the plan I have laid out to pursue, or rather the one God has destined for me . . . And let us hope that in the mysterious ways of the Lord, he will bring about these things we all so much hope for . . . Let us pray that the Lord will completely guide us in all things, and that we may gladly be led by him.[1]

He and Professor Wilson started a Wednesday night prayer group that was so successful they started a second, then a third. They recruited new members every semester by dispatching Christian volunteers to the train station to meet new students, escort them to campus, and help them get oriented.

George threw himself wholeheartedly into every aspect of college life. He entered the college cadet corps, rising in time to captain. Though still slightly built, he joined the football team as a trainer and masseuse. He played the guitar and gave guitar lessons. He became a star member of the Welsh Eccentric Society, devoted to "development in science, literature, and the art of speaking." George gained renown for his elaborate banquet decorations, transforming the dining hall "beyond recognition" with vines and autumn leaves. When the Welsh Eccentric Society and the women's literary club jointly sponsored a reception for the governor of Iowa, each society member was paired with a woman from the club. Since there was no black woman for Carver to escort, his friends arranged for him to escort the governor.

Carver spoke at the organizational meeting of the Iowa State College Agricultural Society in March 1892. For two years he was a delegate to a national YMCA summer program at Lake Geneva, Wisconsin; both summers he was the only black person at the gathering. Four of his paintings were accepted for a statewide exhibition in Cedar Rapids. He was invited to the showing but couldn't afford to go. Hearing the news, his friends took up a collection to buy him a train ticket and a new suit. At least one of his pictures, *Yucca and Cactus*, had the honor of being chosen for display at the 1894 Chicago World's Fair. Carver got to go to Chicago as a member of the Iowa Cadet Honor Guard, escorting the governor on his official visit to the fair. In spite of his artistic success and rank as a cadet officer, he was refused admission to a dinner for cadets at Highland Park Methodist Episcopal Church and later, wearing his cadet uniform, endured shouts of "Nigger!" as he marched.

Carver never mentioned these slurs in his letters to the Milhollands or others, and if they bothered him, he kept his hurt feelings to himself. He applied himself to his studies with customary resolve, earning consistently high grades and impressing his professors with his passion for learning. More and more he began to concentrate on work in the agricultural department, headed by Dr. Louis H. Pammel. Carver coauthored several papers with Dr. Pammel on mycology, the study of mushrooms and other fungus, which was the professor's specialty. In 1894 Carver received his degree from Iowa State, realizing a dream he had worked for nearly all his life.

Immediately he enrolled in a graduate program under Dr. Pammel, though he thought he might also take a painting course at the Chicago Academy of Art. His growing interest in Christianity made him consider enrolling at Moody Bible College as well. He wrote the Milhollands that he was "saving his pennies" in order to take Bible classes and was "praying a great deal" about what to do with his life going forward.[2] Evidently Carver never attended either the art academy or the Bible school. He may well have been too busy with his graduate work, which included teaching freshman biology. Students liked him because he encouraged them to explore and learn from experience rather than getting their learning from the textbook.

As a graduate student George worked as assistant director of the agricultural experiment station under Dr. James Wilson, who had befriended him in his first awkward days at Iowa State. He also studied under Dr. Henry C. Wallace. Both Wilson and Wallace later became U.S. secretaries of agriculture, with Wilson serving sixteen years under three successive presidents, the longest term of any cabinet member in history. Wallace's son, Henry A., was also a secretary of agriculture and vice president under Franklin Roosevelt. Young Henry, who was a boy of six when Carver started his graduate studies, remembered him long afterward as "the kindest, most patient teacher I ever knew. He could cause a little boy to see the things which he saw in a grass flower."[3]

The time was approaching when George would have to decide whether to continue his education and earn a doctorate, begin a teaching career, or take a different path such as those he had considered in painting or Bible studies. He even thought briefly about entering the Christian mission field in Africa. During the fall of 1895, as he began the second and final year of his master's program, Carver was offered a faculty position at Alcorn Agricultural and Mechanical College, a school for blacks in Lorman, Mississippi. In response, Iowa State reappointed Carver as assistant director of the agricultural experiment station at the salary Alcorn offered him. His alma mater hoped he would stay to earn his doctorate and join the faculty there. Professor Wilson wrote the administration at Alcorn, saying Carver was equal to his professors in knowledge and better in "special lines in which he has a taste." Wilson continued:

> We have nobody to take his place and I would never part with a student with so much regret as George Carver . . . I think he feels at home among us, but you call him to go down there and teach agriculture and horticulture to the people of his own race, a people I have been taught to respect . . . I cannot object to his going.[4]

Carver was torn between staying in an environment where he was widely praised and appreciated, and moving to a poor school in the South—where he had never set foot—that would give him the chance to teach other black students. He had triumphed over discrimination in so many ways by the sheer power of his ability and tenacity, and by his natural tendency to see the good in everyone and downplay the disappointments of life. He was comfortable, successful, and assured of a bright future in Iowa. Could he leave it for an unknown future in Mississippi?

While he was considering what to do, Carver got another offer from Tuskegee Institute in Tuskegee, Alabama. Part of the appeal to Carver from Tuskegee's president, Booker T. Washington, was that up to that time Tuskegee had filled all its faculty positions with black men and women. The institute had received money to start an agricultural station and Washington had not found a black person who qualified for the job. If Carver didn't take it, it would mean the school would have to hire a white professor. Washington offered Carver a thousand dollars a year plus board, adding that if that weren't enough, "we shall be willing to do anything in reason that will enable you to decide in favor of coming to Tuskegee."[5]

Carver decided to accept the job at Tuskegee, declaring "the financial feature is satisfactory," and that he would cooperate with Washington "in doing all I can through Christ who strengtheneth me to better the conditions of our people." The men agreed that Carver would finish his master's work, then take up his teaching duties in the fall of 1896. Eager to begin, at

Washington's request he left Iowa State without waiting for the graduation ceremony, packing up his large collection of plant specimens, an expensive microscope given as a farewell gift by the faculty and students, a few paintings, and two of his most treasured possessions: his mother's spinning wheel and her bill of sale to Moses Carver.

≈

George's new employer, Booker Taliaferro Washington, was a gifted and dedicated black educator who overcame daunting obstacles to build a school where blacks could learn a trade to support themselves. Tuskegee made high-quality instruction available even to the poorest blacks, as he himself had once been. Together at Tuskegee, Carver and Washington would make history in the fields of education and race relations in America, though their nineteen-year collaboration was marked by friction between two very strong and very different personalities.

Booker was born the son of a slave and an unidentified white man. His mother's owner recorded his birth in the family Bible on April 5, 1856. By 1860, his mother had married a slave named Washington, yet they lived apart with their respective owners until Emancipation.

After the end of the Civil War, Booker's stepfather reunited the family and moved to Malden, West Virginia, where he found a job packing salt.

Booker's first notion of the value of reading came when he watched his illiterate stepfather write the number "18" in chalk on the head of each salt barrel he packed in order to get credit for the work. Later, his mother got him a copy of the same Webster's blue-backed speller George Carver and millions of other American schoolchildren used during those years. Booker longed to go to school, but his stepfather insisted that the boy work alongside him at the salt spring, and that the family couldn't afford for him to take time off. Eventually Washington relented and let his son go to school, but only if he worked five hours, from 4:00 until 9:00 a.m., before classes started, and then two more hours afterward.

Determined to rise above his circumstances, at age eleven Booker talked his way into a job as houseboy for the salt company owner, General Lewis Ruffner, and his second wife, Viola. In the Ruffner household he learned fine points of etiquette, the art of conversation, and was surrounded by books that further developed his taste for reading and education. In 1872 he traveled alone almost five hundred miles to Hampton Institute in Virginia, arriving on October 5 with fifty cents in cash and his desire for learning undimmed.

Hampton Institute was the vision of General Samuel Chapman Armstrong, born to Presbyterian missionary parents in Hawaii in 1839. General Armstrong's father taught school there for more than thirty years and later became the kingdom's minister of education. Armstrong believed the educational model he had seen in Hawaii—combining traditional education, practical life skills, moral training, and personal hygiene—would work well for emancipated slaves and other blacks. Armstrong founded Hampton in 1869 and, from the beginning, emphasized cleanliness and punctuality as much as science and grammar. Students lined up for personal inspection at 5:45 every morning. Washington had only one suit, which he wore every day to class and to his work as a school janitor, then washed every night. Washington earned his ten-dollar monthly board, and a friend of General Armstrong's paid his seventy-five-dollar annual tuition.

After graduating in 1875, Washington considered becoming a lawyer or a minister, but in the end decided to teach, first back home in West Virginia, then at his alma mater by General Armstrong's invitation, and finally at an experimental school for Native Americans Armstrong had set up at Hampton to help integrate them into white society. Most of the new students had never lived in a building, never slept in a bed, and never used utensils at the table. They especially hated getting their hair cut, giving up smoking, and wearing clothes (particularly underwear). Washington dedicated himself all the more to his work because the popular consensus was that these young men were savages beyond help. He made what he considered great strides with his students, getting them accustomed to wearing white man's clothes, telling them about Christianity, and teaching them to play football.

In May 1881, George W. Campbell, a prominent citizen of Tuskegee, Alabama, had his nephew Moses write to General Armstrong. As part of a political quid-pro-quo, the state had agreed to establish a school for black students in Tuskegee and Campbell wanted to know if any white faculty member at Hampton had the ability and desire to run it. Armstrong recommended Washington, "a graduate of this institution, a very competent capable mulatto, clear headed, modest, sensible, polite and a thorough teacher and superior man. The best man we ever had here. Is his being colored an objection? . . . I am convinced he would not disappoint you. I know of no white man who could do better."[6]

Booker T. Washington was hired and, not surprising, modeled his school after Hampton's style, with an emphasis on punctuality, cleanliness, courtesy, and practical skills. He pawned his gold pocket watch to pay for a brick kiln that supplied not only bricks for buildings at Tuskegee but also found a ready market in the surrounding community. Furthermore, in brick making his students now had a valuable skill. To the boys he also taught farming, carpentry, printing, blacksmithing, and more. The girls had classes in housekeeping, hat making, and sewing. The whole point, from Washington's perspective, was to give black students occupations that would allow them to earn a living wage and make their way in the world. By 1895 Tuskegee enrollment was nearly a thousand, with students from more than twenty states, Africa, and the West Indies. Every student, and every teacher, was black, a point of particular pride for Washington, who built his faculty in the face of admonitions that he'd never find enough qualified black teachers.

In 1896 trustees of the Slater Fund offered to start an agricultural school at Tuskegee. The organization was set up by descendants of Samuel Slater, who emigrated from England in 1768 after memorizing the plans for a revolutionary machine that manufactured cotton thread. Reproducing the machines in America, Slater made a fortune in the textile industry. In 1882 his heirs established a fund in New York for the Christian education of emancipated slaves with an endowment of one million dollars. Washington was delighted at the idea of an agricultural school because it offered his students yet another way of supporting themselves. Knowledge of crop breeding, planting cycles, fertilizing, soil conservation, budgeting, and marketing their harvest improved the chances that black farmers would move up from their usual status as landless sharecroppers or field hands to owning farms of their own. It was the kind of bootstrap program Washington strongly encouraged—free black men and women lifting themselves out of poverty without handouts or condescending help from the white establishment.

Slater trustees suggested off the record that Washington find a white man to head the new school, since they knew of "no colored man in the country fitted for such work." Washington took that as a challenge. His research led him to the only black graduate student at Iowa Agricultural College. In recruiting George Carver, Washington consciously played on his racial identity. "If we cannot secure you," he wrote, "we shall be forced perhaps to put in a white man."[7] He also promised that the new facilities built with the Slater Fund gift would be unsurpassed in the country.

After Carver accepted the Tuskegee offer, Washington persuaded him to skip his November 10 graduation ceremony to be at Tuskegee at the beginning of the semester. Classes had already begun, however, when Carver arrived on October 8, 1896, with visions of heading the greatest agricultural research facility in the country. He felt he had a lifetime of experience and accomplishment to bring to the task. Wherever he had gone in the past, from the wilderness of western Kansas to the halls of Iowa State, he had been a standout who earned the admiration and praise of everyone who knew him. He was accustomed to success and fond of compliments, and expected both to continue at Tuskegee. Circumstances soon proved otherwise.

PRESSURES AND
POLITICS

George Washington Carver and Booker T. Washington were in many ways cut from the same cloth. Both overcame incredible hardship to get an education. Both were passionate about learning and handing down their knowledge to others. They accepted inferior treatment because of their race, while at the same time seizing every opportunity to demonstrate their abilities. Yet for all their apparent similarities, Carver and his new employer were very different men from very different worlds.

Carver lived much of his life in white society as a respected and admired oddity. He was long accustomed to being the center of attention. His life revolved around scientific study and research, painting and drawing, music, refined conversation, and the joy of learning for learning's sake. Booker T. Washington, on the other hand, lived in a world dedicated to practicality and common sense. Tuskegee in its early years didn't even offer college-level classes. The focus was on vocational training, income-producing skills leading to self-sufficiency, and simple agricultural techniques and budgeting practices that yielded crop surpluses, independence from the sharecropper system, and a measure of financial stability.

The two men's personalities were polar opposites as well. Washington spent part of every year raising money in the parlors of New York and New England millionaires. He moved comfortably in circles that included Andrew Carnegie, John D. Rockefeller, and other industrial titans. (Years later he would dine at the White House with President Theodore Roosevelt and his family.) He was a captivating orator whose electrifying speech on racial harmony at the 1894 Cotton States Exposition drew national headlines. His rich, cultivated voice and patrician accent were those of the Virginia aristocracy. Carver by contrast was far more comfortable in the classroom or surrounded by a group of friends than in a public forum. His feminine-sounding voice was soft and weak. He was thin and delicate looking, especially next to the robust, kinetic, powerful figure of Washington.

The years from the time Carver arrived at Tuskegee until Booker T. Washington's death in 1915 were one of the most productive—and most infuriating—periods in Carver's life. The tension between the two men surfaced almost immediately. Carver arrived after years at a well-funded, well-equipped state university, assuming his teaching and publishing credentials had already earned him a place of high honor at Tuskegee, which, after all, had come looking for him and not the other way around.

He was surprised and irritated to discover that, like all the other bachelor teachers, he would live with a roommate in the teachers' dormitory. There was no place for his large collection of plant specimens, books, and other materials. And though he evidently thought the Slater Fund had already given money for his laboratory, there was no lab, no equipment, no assistants to help him, and no course of study in place for the agricultural institute. The situation prompted him to reconsider choosing science over art, as he made clear in a curt letter to the school finance committee on November 27, 1896, requesting more room.

> I do not expect to teach many years, but will quit as soon as I can trust my work to others, and engage in my brush work, which will be of great honor to our people . . . At present I have no room even to unpack my goods. I beg you to give me these, and suitable ones also . . . At the present the room is full of mice and they are into my boxes doing me much damage I fear. While I am with you please fix me so I may be of as much service to you as possible . . . I am handicapped in my work.[1]

Carver got more space: a private office in one of the main buildings plus two residential rooms in the boys' dormitory. His high airs and complaints made some of Carver's new colleagues resent him from the first. His salary was more than twice the school average, even though he had no family to support. His demand for more space seemed self-centered and arrogant. Most of the faculty were young mulatto men in the Booker Washington mold, always impeccably dressed, sticklers for decorum, cleanliness, and punctuality, concentrating on practical vocational skills, endlessly scrambling for money to keep the school going and assist its overwhelmingly poor, rural students.

Carver's first assignment was to take charge of the campus dairy. This in-house operation had the twofold benefit of teaching students how to be dairy farmers and supplying the dining hall with milk, butter, and cream. Washington believed that in order for the process to run smoothly he needed daily reports from the dairy department on the volume of products produced. That way the dining hall manager would know if he had to buy any extra that day. Reports also showed the students' progress and monitored the health of the animals. Washington expected complete and accurate reports at a certain time every morning.

None of this fit with Carver's idea of his position on the faculty. He enjoyed teaching the students and was willing to supervise care of the dairy herd, but he bristled at writing reports. He also had to cope with the fact that his students were just learning their work and often made mistakes or did things inefficiently. This caused delays in delivering the milk or making the butter, and consequent delays in delivering the reports. When Washington pressed him to finish his reports on time, Carver complained that he had all he could do handling the students and the animals, and that he had no secretary to help with the paperwork so had to write everything himself.

Washington had little patience with complainers. His response was to add to Carver's workload, putting him in charge of building and maintaining fences and collecting hooves from slaughtered animals to make harness oil, among other jobs. Carver grudgingly shouldered these tasks. Before long he assumed an attitude that reflected an odd combination of dissatisfaction and contentment. As long as Washington was alive Carver chafed under the burdens of paperwork, punctuality, and the feeling he was underappreciated. Yet at the same time he nurtured a great love of teaching and took joy in his students and in the many agricultural experiments and programs he pursued.

One of Carver's shining successes early on was a series of agricultural bulletins funded by a small state grant. The idea was to conduct agricultural research, then present the results as practical advice to local farmers in simple language. The first agricultural bulletin he produced, "Feeding Acorns," advised farmers to mix wild acorns with the corn they fed to livestock in order to stretch expensive corn and to make use of acorns that would otherwise go to waste. His research showed that chickens laid more eggs and cows produced more milk when fed the cheaper mixture.

The second bulletin, "Experiments with Sweet Potatoes," advised farmers to fertilize their sweet potato patches with a certain combination of phosphate and potash. A one-tenth acre test plot with no fertilizer produced small potatoes worth 25¢ a bushel at a yield of 40 bushels per acre. The phosphate/potash plot produced potatoes worth 50¢ a bushel at a yield of 266 bushels per acre. The potatoes from the first test plot netted $2.50; those from the second plot, after deducting the cost of chemicals, netted $121.00.

The agricultural bulletins won high praise from black and white farmers alike. The publications satisfied Carver's passion for research and experimentation, Washington's for practical application, and both men's desire to help black families become financially independent. Iowa State praised the bulletins in print, as did Auburn University and Mississippi State, adding fuel to the fire of Carver's argument that he was underappreciated at Tuskegee. If Washington and the institute's administration acknowledged Carver's success, they also expected him to be about his work. Washington regularly reminded Carver that his organizational skills still needed improvement. As far as the institute's president was concerned, a surplus of achievement in one area did not offset a deficiency in another.

Carver resented it whenever others presumed to tell him how to do his job. He was the one doing the work, the supposed expert, and wanted to be left alone. In a memo to Washington he wrote, "I think it ludicrously unfair to have persons sit in an office and dictate what I have to do and how I can do it. If I thought things were to run as they have always run I would not stay here any longer than I could get away."[2] Over the years Carver would threaten repeatedly to leave Tuskegee, to the point where it lost all sense of impact.

Carver and Washington could be extremely cordial to each other, and Carver often commented on how happy he was to be helping "his people" at Tuskegee. Nonetheless, Washington's insistence on procedure and exactitude clashed constantly with Carver's disorganized state and his disdain for administrative routine. The dairy reports remained a bone of contention. Carver pleaded that he had too much to do to fill out paperwork, that he had to take time to correct other people's mistakes, and that calving cows couldn't stick to a schedule.

Washington was unconvinced. In a memo to Carver he insisted, "I want the milk report every morning, and on it I want the number of cows milked . . . I must insist that it be sent promptly each morning and marked as I have directed." Another time Washington added that "some of the students at the dairy barn complain that they are working now fifteen and sixteen hours a day. If this is true it is entirely too much, and the number of hours should be reduced to ten or something near that."[3]

Other memos referenced faulty door fasteners on the dairy wagon, and farm machinery left out in the rain. Washington missed nothing, and anything that smacked of waste or inattention generated an immediate memo.

Carver chafed at Washington's methods while admiring him as an educator and black leader. Around this time, he wrote one of the many flattering notes he penned to Washington over the years. "Among both black & white you are living several hundred years ahead of the common herd of both races . . . 3 or 4 hundred years from now people will know and honor your greatness more than now because they will have been educated up to it." He also reported enthusiastically that fall that the "students & teachers have all the green peas they can use, cabbage, tomatoes, squash, some green corn, watermelons, cantaloupes, cucumbers, peaches, grapes, and will soon have sweet potatoes. The teachers have all the honey they can use judiciously."[4] Though the dairy had its problems, the agricultural program overall was a tremendous success in keeping dining room costs under control while putting institute land to productive use and training a new generation of farmers.

In 1897 Tuskegee completed the agricultural building Carver had expected and lobbied for since his arrival. His former professor at Iowa, James Wilson, accepted his invitation to attend the opening ceremonies. Wilson was appointed secretary of agriculture by President William McKinley and accompanied the president on a visit to Tuskegee the next year. On December 16, 1898, the president and Mrs. McKinley, most of the cabinet, and a group of generals from the recent Spanish-American War came to the campus. White residents of the town of Tuskegee were agog with excitement, many of them offering their help to plan the welcoming festivities at the black school, some on the condition that they remain anonymous. The parade organized for their distinguished guests took an hour and a half to go by. The only record of Carver's involvement is a memo from Washington putting him in charge of repainting all the farm machinery used in the parade.

Carver must have felt that before he could get one responsibility under control, Washington was adding another to it. In time Carver was put in charge of maintaining the wells, drainage ditches, and toilet facilities on campus, finding a site for a new peach orchard, and endlessly maintaining school equipment and property. Washington believed blacks had to be more tidy and better organized to get the same level of respect as whites. He was therefore determined that everything a visitor on campus might see was in perfect condition all the time. He put Carver in charge of repairing wagons, cleaning up stray branches, and a long list of other jobs.

For all the problems he had with the administration, Carver was a popular teacher and also found many admirers among the county's white population. Shy though he was, Carver made friends easily because one-on-one he was so kindhearted and always interested in what others were doing. Not long after he settled in Tuskegee, he was out collecting plant specimens when a white woman stopped him and asked if he was a peddler. He explained he was looking for plant diseases and insects harmful to plants in order to study ways to prevent them. She asked him to come look at her failing roses. "I showed her just what to do for them," he told Washington later, "in fact, sat down and wrote it out for her."[5] Carver's reputation as a plant doctor grew rapidly, so that before long he welcomed a steady stream of amateur gardeners asking for advice.

By 1902 Carver had settled into a familiar routine at Tuskegee. He spent part of every day teaching agriculture and chemistry classes, oversaw a hundred seventy acres of experimental crop fields, ran the dairy, and also supervised a poultry farm Washington started in order to give girls another vocational skill. A new library had been built with a gift from Andrew Carnegie, and the school gave Carver two rooms in the old library for living and storage space; he thought he might convert part of the new area into a painting studio. His agricultural bulletins continued to be extremely popular, with requests coming from Cuba, Mexico, and other countries as far away as India.

Professor Carver had embraced Tuskegee's emphasis on economy by developing paint pigment from clay in a drainage ditch; finding innovative uses for inexpensive and prolific black-eyed peas, including a coffee substitute; and buying a bone mill so students could mix their own fertilizer instead of burning livestock carcasses while buying calcium meal. When Washington suggested the dairy department start making cheese as well as its other products, Carver proved it would be more expensive to make cheese than to keep buying it.

On the administrative side, Carver never seemed to improve his performance nor Washington to relax his standards, so that the friction there continued. Early on, Carver looked forward to Washington's long absences on fund-raising tours, expecting a break from the college president's relentless rules and standards. Unfortunately for him, Washington insisted that Carver send regular detailed reports to him on the road. Washington's brother, John, was now general superintendent of industries, and took charge in Booker's absence, adding his own criticisms and memos on everything from Carver letting his workers quit too soon before supper to leaving a harness out in the rain where campus visitors could see it.

Carver constantly reminded the administration that his staff and budget were too small to carry out all the projects they expected him to do plus write reports about them. It seemed promising, then, when in 1902 George R. Bridgeforth joined the faculty to assist Professor Carver at the agricultural institute. Where Carver was scattered and inattentive in administrative matters, Bridgeforth was precise and observant. The new hire might have been the liaison with Washington and the school administration that Carver so badly needed. Instead, he quickly became a rival, scoring political points with administrators at Carver's expense, taking the initiative in making and implementing his own decisions, and openly criticizing Carver.

Carver had not done well managing the chicken yard, and quickly handed that annoying responsibility off to Bridgeforth. When conditions failed to improve, the job was reassigned to a young institute worker named Columbus Barrows under Carver's supervision. What followed was a replay of the dairy farm story: Carver was too busy with what he considered more important work to see to every detail of raising chickens; he was understaffed and the people he had, he considered green and incompetent. Washington meanwhile sent a steady stream of memos expressing his concern about low egg production, the number of dead chickens, an untidy chicken yard, and incomplete or late reports on the operation.

Bridgeforth took advantage of the opportunity to highlight Carver's shortcomings in memos of his own to Washington. For his part, Washington still couldn't understand why a task so seemingly simple as raising chickens could cause such a fuss, and why his suggestions and directives were repeatedly ignored. He also took note of the eager, energetic, cooperative, and ambitious Bridgeforth.

Around this time Carver received an unsolicited job offer from Knoxville College, a school in Tennessee for black students whose white president, Ralph W. McGranaham, offered a faculty post teaching both agriculture and art. Tempted as he was to leave his frustrations behind for new opportunities, Carver didn't know what to do. He wrote his friend and former professor, Secretary of Agriculture James Wilson, for advice.

"Don't do it," Wilson advised. "They can not spare you there yet, and the work you are doing in helping to educate future teachers is the best work you are doing and the best work Tuskegee is doing; and you should stick right to it." The secretary continued, "I hope the Tuskegee people will fully appreciate your value along these lines. But stay by Mr. Washington. He is doing a work that should be duplicated in many other places, not only for the colored people but also for the white." Perceptive and encouraging, he added, "I hope I live to see the day when white people will be regarded as good as colored folks along these lines."[6]

No doubt Washington genuinely admired Carver's dedication and ability. He included a flattering description of the professor in an article he wrote for the *Atlantic Monthly* magazine in the fall of 1903. The piece delighted Carver because he took it as a sign that Washington appreciated him even in the face of all his criticism. Yet in May 1904 Washington ordered a formal investigation into the struggling poultry yard operations. On September 22, the investigative committee reported its findings to the executive council. Since all department heads were *ex officio* members of the council and Carver headed the agricultural school, he was likely in the room for a scathing report on an operation the committee declared was in "very bad condition." They concluded that the daily poultry reports were falsified. When large numbers of chickens died, Carver had warned Columbus Barrows not to report them all at once, but spread them out over time so Washington would be less likely to notice. Carver had also tried to cover up the high death rate by not reporting some of them at all and buying replacement chickens with his own money instead.

Bridgeforth and other agricultural department staff suggested that their department be reorganized under John Washington with Carver as head of the agricultural experiment station and instruction, and Bridgeforth as director of agricultural industries. There would be no official department head per se. Carver was embarrassed, belittled, and stung by the committee report and by Bridgeforth's suggestions. He wrote to Washington on October 14, his passion evident in the way his writing scrawled across the page. This was, he said,

> the most painful experience of my life. For seven years I have labored with you: have built up one of the best Agl. laboratories in the south . . . The museum is the best of its kind in the south and constantly growing. The Experiment Station . . . I am sure has no equal in the south. Now to be branded as a liar and party to such hellish deception is more than I can bear, and if your committee feel that I have willfully lied or party to such lies as were told my resignation is at your disposal.[7]

Washington at this point made a very wise move. He suggested that Carver talk with Washington's wife, Margaret, about the "unfortunate occurrence of recent date." Margaret asked Carver to reconsider resigning. While there is no record of their discussion, she doubtless knew Carver's value to the institution, understood his wounded feelings, and could approach the matter in a more conciliatory tone than her husband could.

By October 19 Carver had calmed down and softened his stance. To Washington he wrote, "If the school brands me as a liar and party to such hellish deceptions it would be best for me to go, my usefulness to Tuskegee would be at an end." Yet by the end of his three-page letter, he affirmed, "If you have faith in me I will take hold of the [poultry] yard with renewed vigor and give you some chickens, a number that you will be proud of. If your committee wishes to retain me on these terms I assure you I shall give them honest, faithful service and never let such an error creep in again."[8]

Carver withdrew the olive branch, however, after Washington told him on November 3 that his new title would be, as previously proposed, director of the experiment station and agricultural instruction rather than director of agriculture. The professor was affronted, insisting the change in title was "too far a drop downward," and, despite his frequent complaint of being overworked, said that his responsibilities could not be divided between himself and Bridgeforth. He asked that Washington "kindly accept my resignation to take effect just as soon as I can get the herbarium and cabinets labeled and in place where they will be of the highest service to the school."[9]

Within the week Carver had altered his stance again, saying that "if there is to be no Dept. head I should bear, at least, an advisory relationship to it," that his suggestions on various matters ought to be considered more carefully, and that he needed a stenographer half a day. "I think this is due me," he declared.[10] Carver had to face the fact that henceforth he would share control of Tuskegee's agricultural program with George Bridgeforth and that both of them would answer to John Washington. Carver felt slighted, underappreciated, and misunderstood by his bosses. As strong as these feelings were, they were more than offset by his love of teaching, agricultural experimentation, and the joy of seeing his students succeed.

Carver and Washington often received letters from graduates who had done well: a bricklayer who got a job three days after returning home; a woman graduate teaching poultry farming and getting top price for her hens. Employers wrote seeking Tuskegee graduates for their workforce. Manufacturers sent Carver farm machinery to assess, donating a sample of the item in exchange for his critique. To his delight, he received a steady stream of offers to submit scientific papers both in America and abroad, especially Germany, world famous at the turn of the twentieth century for its scientific excellence.

The next decade for George Washington Carver would be filled with more of the joys and frustrations of his first years at Tuskegee: growing scientific and educational success with a reputation to match, contrasted with ongoing bureaucratic frustration and departmental turf wars. As his star rose in the fields of agricultural research and teaching, the misery of the poultry yard was never far away.

FROM POWER TO POWER

Part of Carver's ongoing problem with Booker T. Washington and the administrative process at Tuskegee was that Carver was transparently delighted about subjects or tasks he enjoyed, and equally transparent in resisting work he disliked or that he thought compromised his dignity, position, or sense of self-worth.

What Carver loved most, as he had since he was a boy, was studying plants. He spent long hours ambling through the woods around campus collecting specimens, then cataloging, preserving, and experimenting with them in his office. He sometimes carried colored pencils with him and would make sketches along the way in the margins or backs of whatever stray pages he happened to have with him. At the university he tended a huge collection of living plants as well, his "plant museum" or "herbarium," stuffed with specimens that interested him or that he enjoyed looking at.

Most days Carver worked at the experimental station, where

he monitored assorted strains of crops that varied according to the type of experiment he was conducting. One departmental report listed a hundred acres of sweet potatoes and forty acres of black-eyed peas under cultivation, plus smaller plots of onions, collard greens, turnips, beets, beans, squash, lettuce, and radishes. Professor Carver determined what combinations of fertilizer and other additives produced the best yield, and developed as many uses for the crop as possible so nothing would be wasted and the farmer would get the maximum benefit from his labor and investment.

Carver also enjoyed sharing what he learned with as many people as possible, both out of appreciation for nature and as a means of fulfilling his goal to help blacks live more fulfilling and independent lives. Many of them struggled as sharecroppers, working their employers' land in exchange for a share of the crop, or as tenants farming rented acreage. Carver wanted to improve their crop yield enough so they could afford their own farms, decent homes for their families, and modern equipment to make their lives less wearisome while improving production even more.

Professor Carver's research had produced a wealth of practical information that could help the family farmer of modest means. In addition to his advice on fertilizer and soil additives, he encouraged crop rotation and soil conservation techniques. He showed farmers how to reduce erosion of fertile topsoil by plowing their crop rows in a way that kept rain from washing it away. He taught them to plant peanuts and beans in rotation to add nitrogen to the soil that other crops took out.

Another goal Carver set was to find a substitute for "king cotton," the most important cash crop in the South and, in many communities, the foundation of the entire economy. Cotton is hard on the soil and, until automated equipment became widespread in the 1950s, required endless, diligent, backbreaking labor. Healthy plants had to be thinned and weeded by hand with hoes—the process of "chopping cotton" that had consumed slaves' working days for decades on end—then harvested by hand, one individual boll at a time picked and dropped into the long cloth sacks that cotton pickers trailed behind them.

Carver wanted to offer small farmers an alternative to cotton that was easier on the soil and required less relentless physical labor. Adding to Carver's sense of urgency was that in 1894 the boll weevil had crossed the Rio Grande from Mexico and was creeping northward, evidently unstoppable. This was a small beetle that ate cotton bolls, destroying a field and a year's work within days. Carver and other scientists knew the boll weevil would arrive in eastern Alabama eventually. George wanted to have an alternative crop ready to propose. But to be successful, the cotton substitute had to have a ready and reliable market. No farmer would want to risk his year's income on an unfamiliar crop with an unknown level of demand.

Carver thought black-eyed peas, which he and others at Tuskegee called "cow peas," showed promise not only as a food but also as a flour substitute, coffee substitute, and as animal feed. It was sweet potatoes, however, that he believed would be the best cash crop replacement for cotton, and the more uses he could find for them, the more likely he believed farmers would be to plant them. From the sweet potato or its vine he developed a range of food items including candy, molasses, and breakfast cereal, plus substitutes for flour, sugar, coconut, tapioca, ginger, chocolate, yeast, coffee, and vinegar. He also produced sweet potato dyes, paints, library paste, ink, shoe polish, paper, and much more.

Carver had long demonstrated his interest in conducting useful and practical research, and in sharing it with as many people as possible. The agricultural bulletins were early examples that led to other beneficial programs. Tuskegee began hosting its Farmer's Conferences in 1892. These annual meetings, held on campus, were forums for local farmers to share stories about their problems and successes. Attendance grew steadily, especially after Carver arrived and his reputation grew. The event expanded to two days, the first for the farmers to talk and the second for educators, ministers, and other leaders to give them encouragement and advice. In time both black and white farmers, some traveling long distances from the North, flocked to the gatherings. One black farmer wrote to the school that he was twenty, destitute, and lame at the time of Emancipation and now owned thirteen hundred acres of land. Another participant wrote, "I thank God on my knees for these Conferences. They are giving us homes."[1]

In 1898 Tuskegee added a Farmer's Institute Fair, giving farmers a forum for displaying their crops, livestock, and homemade products from cross stitching to canned goods. The event was such a success that in 1911 it was combined with the

Macon County Fair, though there were separate ticket booths, food stalls, and other facilities for whites and blacks.

In 1904 Professor Carver staged a free six-week lecture course for farmers during January and February when work in the fields was light. Shortened to two weeks ahead of the annual Farmer's Institute Fair and officially named the Short Course in Agriculture, it became another means for Carver and the institute's faculty to answer questions, offer advice, and demonstrate techniques for improving farm yields and profits.

One of Carver's most popular and enduring outreach efforts was a portable display and demonstration setup on wheels known as the Jessup Wagon. The idea started with a suggestion from Booker Washington that Carver design a wagon that could be equipped as a traveling agricultural school. Popular as the Farmer's Institute Fair and associated events were, there were many farmers who lacked the time or money to attend them, or who didn't know about them. Carver's agricultural bulletins continued to be extremely popular, with requests for copies always outstripping his miniscule printing budget, yet more than half of Southern blacks were illiterate. Professor Carver wanted to make sure they were not left behind.

The professor sketched a design for a wagon that student carpenters and wheelwrights could build, with fold-up sides that opened to display charts on soil improvement, stock raising, and other farm work, plus samples of farm equipment for demonstration. It was a classroom on wheels a teacher could transport directly to working farmers in the field. New York philanthropist Morris K. Jessup, a member of the Slater Fund's board of directors, donated money to build and operate the wagon, and in 1906 the first Jessup Wagon took to the road, traveling to whatever crossroads or country store, farm or field its audience could reach. The first summer, more than two thousand people a month attended Jessup Wagon presentations. Its success was somewhat bittersweet for Carver. Though he had designed and outfitted the wagon, it was Bridgeforth who took it out on its rounds.

For all the effort Carver made to get practical information into the hands of farmers who needed it, that work never overshadowed his love for teaching. Professor Carver complained at times about his teaching load or having to teach at all in addition to his various other responsibilities at the school. Judging by what he said and wrote, however, and by his students' reaction to him, George Washington Carver was a brilliant and inspired teacher who felt a special calling to the field. Generations of students would say he transformed their lives.

Carver believed that direct observation and hands-on experience were essential to learning. He also believed that students learned about botany by studying other subjects, some of which seemed completely unrelated to plants. Carver often brought plant samples or results of his experiments into the classroom. Rather than using textbooks, he emphasized seeing and examining plants. Rather than telling his students a set of facts, he had them derive the facts for themselves. He wasn't there to spoonfeed his students, but rather to encourage and guide them on their own journeys of self discovery. In an introduction to a booklet published at Tuskegee in 1902, Carver wrote that every teacher should realize that a very large proportion of every student's work must lie outside the class room . . . The study of Nature is both entertaining and instructive, and it is the only true method that leads up to a clear understanding of the great natural principles which surround every branch of business in which we may engage. Aside from this, it encourages investigation and stimulates originality.

In another brochure he added that the

thoughtful educator . . . also understands that the most effective and lasting education is the one that makes the pupil handle, discuss and familiarize himself with real things about him, of which the majority are surprisingly ignorant.[2]

Since he lived in the boys' dormitory, Rockefeller Hall, Carver came in contact with many students who had no classes at all in his department. And even as his teaching load declined over the years, he never missed a chance to share his interest in the natural world with them outside of class, or to encourage and help them in ways that had nothing to do with academics. Tuskegee students were the grandchildren of slaves. Desperately poor, often from unstable families, they were woefully unprepared for the work ahead of them. They were homesick, afraid, worried about keeping up with their classmates. Carver was a tenderhearted mentor who took a sincere personal interest in these students. No doubt he saw himself in their eyes and his story in their struggles. Word spread through each new class that Professor Carver was a kind, approachable man, a good listener who gave wise advice. One student wrote, "When advice is sought by the humblest student there is no 'red tape' to encounter in entering his office."[3]

Carver guided students through the bureaucracy of the school and advised them on other problems. He helped a disabled student get his hospital bill reduced. He gave counsel on marriage (to wait until you're ready—"get your bird cage before you take unto yourself your canary") and recommended that a young man or woman be "as wise as a serpent and as harmless as a dove." He encouraged them to work hard and make a difference in the world, never be afraid of innovative ideas, and faithfully follow their dreams. He told them to look neither "up to the rich or down on the poor," but to be one who "takes his share of the world and lets other people have theirs."[4]

The professor also loaned many students money and cosigned loans for others. He didn't believe in giving money away because he thought it robbed students of their initiative, but he helped struggling boys and girls who had already sacrificed so much to get to Tuskegee, so that they could stay. Tuition was free, but room and board cost $8.50 per term, and there were other expenses for uniforms and various supplies. Carver evidently had ready money to loan. He had neither asked for nor received a raise since he arrived. But he lived on campus, wore rumpled lab coats and smocks—some of which he made himself—and spent almost nothing. Though he had been a dandy as a younger man, sporting fine clothes and an impressive waxed mustache, he gradually lost interest in his looks, adapting the style of the classic absent-minded professor. Some months he stuck his paycheck in a coat pocket and forgot about it for weeks until the accounting office asked him to cash it. Despite his rule about giving money, he did give cash gifts to students he thought needed and deserved them, and once donated a piano to the girls' dormitory.

Tuskegee was a showplace of black initiative and accomplishment, yet Carver knew his students had come from a world where discrimination was the law of the land, and to that world they would return. He never missed an opportunity to encourage them not to be defeated by the circumstances of their race, but to prove themselves worthy of respect and never to answer bitterness with bitterness.

He wrote,

When our thoughts—which bring actions—are filled with hate against anyone, Negro or white, we are in a living hell. That is as real as hell will ever be. While hate for our fellow man puts us in a living hell, holding good thoughts for them brings us an opposite state of living, one of happiness, success, peace. We are then in heaven.[5]

Scientist and master's graduate that he was, Carver never embraced the scientific method, whereby a researcher meticulously compared one experiment with another that was different in only one detail; if the outcome was different, that detail was the cause. Instead, Carver took a subjective, intuitive approach to research. This may have been in part because botany had been so important to him from so young an age. He observed and experimented with plants long before he knew anything about formal procedures. It was also because George Carver saw the handiwork of the Creator God in every leaf and stem and vine. There was a miraculous aspect to the world that defied quantifiable scientific precision.

Thanks to the Carvers and the Milhollands, and to his own pursuit of faith, Carver became a devout Christian as a young man. He knew that some scientists and others scoffed at the idea of a supreme being creating the physical world out of nothing. It had to evolve, they said, or be developed slowly through natural processes. Carver believed just the opposite: the more he learned about the beauty, complexity, and interconnectedness of the world, the more convinced he was that it could only have been formed supernaturally, by the hand of God.

Carver often talked about the Creator in the classroom. He told his students that the more they knew about plants and the rest of the natural world, the more they could know about the Creator who made those things—and made the students as well. Some days his botany lectures were more impromptu sermon than science lesson. His sincerity and conviction carried over to his students, who responded excitedly both to the idea of God as Creator and to the thought that God could have actually made each of them. Religion suddenly had a new relevance, a new immediacy.

In 1907 Carver was asked to teach a Bible study on Sunday night after supper. The suggestion came from a student or a lab assistant, either of whom would have been well aware of

Carver's faith and his willingness to share it. The professor agreed, and was pleased to see about fifty boys come to his first session, held in a room at the library. Carver didn't talk about theology or Bible history but about the magnificent natural creations God fashioned and that anyone could study and appreciate. He illustrated his talks with plant samples, drawings, maps, and other interesting examples. Within three months, attendance averaged more than a hundred. Even though Sunday after supper was one of the few unstructured times of the week at Tuskegee, students bolted down their meals and hurried to the library to get a seat. Latecomers stood outside at the open windows to hear the professor's lesson.

In his Sunday classes, as in his weekday classroom lectures, Carver returned time and again to the connection between the natural world and its Creator. As he expressed it in a letter to a student:

> To me nature in its varied forms are the little windows through which God permits me to commune with him, and to see much of his glory, by simply lifting the curtain, and looking in. I love to think of nature as wireless telegraph stations through which God speaks to us every day, every hour, and every moment of our lives.[6]

Professor Carver was by now one of the most popular professors on campus. His teaching style nurtured a sense of discovery and excitement. Rather than a dry recitation of facts, Carver continually encouraged his students to learn for themselves and to appreciate the beautiful, useful world the Creator had made for them. He also continued to lavish attention on students outside the classroom, encouraging them in their schoolwork, helping them financially, and giving them advice on personal matters. He kept in touch with many of them after they graduated, exchanging letters through the years about new jobs, new families, new triumphs and challenges.

In 1910 Sir Harry Johnson met Professor Carver during a visit to Tuskegee. Johnson was a British botanist who also played a key political role in the colonization of Africa. In his book *The Negro in the New World*, Sir Harry wrote of his impression of Carver:

> He is, as regards complexion and features, an absolute Negro; but in the cut of his clothes, the accents of his speech, the soundness of his science, he might be a professor of Botany not at Tuskegee, but Oxford or Cambridge. Any European botanist of distinction, after ten minutes' conversation with this man, instinctively would deal with him "de puissance en puissance."

The French means literally "from power to power," the sense being that a European scholar would treat Carver as his equal. Sir Harry said little about Carver's achievements in improving the lot of black farmers in the American South, concentrating instead on Carver's high standing with Secretary of Agriculture Wilson and other prominent whites. Sir Harry added,

I have always said that the best means . . . for destroying race prejudice is to make [oneself] a useful, and if possible, an indispensable member of the community in which he lives. I do not know of a better illustration of this than may be found in the case of Professor Carver.[7]

Booker T. Washington worked tirelessly to raise the profile and the standing of Tuskegee in the public eye. To the extent that Sir Harry's words enhanced the school's reputation, Washington was pleased. Sir Harry's remarks also reminded Washington that despite his idiosyncrasies, Carver was a gifted teacher and a tireless and brilliant researcher whose star shone bright even to such a world traveler and expert observer as Sir Harry.

But the curse of the poultry yard still remained. An inquiry in the fall of 1910 found that 765 chickens were unaccounted for. John Washington and George Bridgeforth proposed that the industrial and teaching divisions of the agriculture department, which had been separated in 1904 partly to allow Carver to save face and keep the appearance of departmental control, be recombined into one department under Bridgeforth. The reorganization went into effect in October 1910. On November 19, Carver again tendered his resignation.

Washington did not want Carver to go now, any more than he had wanted him to go when the professor had threatened to resign earlier. Washington would not willingly lose so talented and capable a faculty member, and tried yet again to place him in a position where his abilities could be applied and his shortcomings be as little of a liability to Tuskegee as possible. Washington knew better than anyone that Carver had a very fragile ego; he fished often for compliments and felt misunderstood and unappreciated when he didn't get them. The professor was a man with rare and wonderful gifts, accompanied by stubbornness and pride that made him a hard man to manage. Washington persevered. On November 22 he sent Professor Carver a counterproposal that would establish a Department of Research with Carver as head, excuse him from classroom teaching in the academic department, and promise a "first class laboratory to be fitted up, so as to enable him to carry out whatever investigations he may wish to undertake . . ."[8]

Professor Carver withdrew his letter of resignation for the moment, but was unhappy again by February of the next year, insisting to Washington that "the new Department is not going to receive the sympathy or support of the school . . . I am not satisfied and cannot be under the existing conditions."[9] He also still didn't have his laboratory.

Washington replied with a five-page letter touching on every point of contention between Carver and the administration. Clearly the president of Tuskegee was trying to settle matters once and for all. He wrote in part:

> Perhaps in the past we have done ourselves as well as you an injustice by pursuing a policy of trying to please everybody. This policy has not resulted in success . . . We cannot stand any further or pursue a policy which permits you or anyone else to argue at length every order that is given, and to lay down the conditions upon which you will [carry them out] . . .

When it comes to the organization of classes, the ability required to secure a properly organized and large school or section of a school, you are wanting in ability. When it comes to the matter of practical farm management which will secure definite, practical, financial results, you are wanting again in ability. You are not to be blamed for this. It is very rare that one individual anywhere combines all the elements of success. You are a great teacher, a great lecturer, a great inspirer of young men and old men . . . we have been trying as best we could to help you do the work for which you are best fitted and to leave aside that for which you are least fitted.

I was greatly surprised . . . to find that you wish a laboratory fitted up for your exclusive use and that you do not mean to give instruction to any student in this laboratory . . . We have no right to expend so large a sum of money in the fitting up of a laboratory which is not to be used as frequently as possible in the instruction of students.

You seem to have made up your mind that you are to give no instruction; that you are to teach no classes whatever. Here again, the school cannot agree . . .

You do not help yourself when you assume the attitude that when you make a request . . . that the last dollar you request for chemicals, etc., shall be spent, nothing must be cut down, that you must have all or nothing: that is an attitude, again, which the school cannot comply with.

My own requests for supplies go before the Finance Committee the same as yours. Very often the Finance

Committee refuses to give me what I want. The same is true
for every officer of the institution . . .

I repeat that all of us recognize your great ability, recognize your rare talents in certain directions, and we should be
sorry to part with your service, but the time has now come for
perfect frankness and for definite action.[10]

A letter from Secretary Wilson to Carver on December 10
was encouraging and congratulatory. Far from being a slight or
a rebuke, Carver's former professor considered the administrative change a step forward. He was "very much pleased," he
wrote, "to find that you have been promoted to a higher class
of work." He went on:

Research, of course, is the highest class of work connected
with agriculture. Your abilities that were brought out through
your education at Ames are now fully recognized and it will
place you in the corps of experimenters of the whole country and the whole world. I have no hesitation in concluding
that you will add to the sum of human knowledge along these
lines, very materially and very promptly.[11]

Placated for the time being, Carver chafed nonetheless at
the seemingly endless delays in completing his new laboratory.
Then he complained of not having a budget for equipment, telling Washington that his mind was "not in condition to do good
work, and if it was I could not do it because I have nothing to
do it with."[12]

As the sparring continued through the next school year, Washington tried once more to put an end to Carver's dissatisfaction and perceived slights. On June 12, 1912, he wrote

Professor Carver:

From now on until further notice I think it well for you to understand that your work will consist of the following:

1. In charge of the Experiment Station.
2. Poultry Yard.
3. Research.
4. Teaching agriculture or botany in the Academic Department [under Bridgeforth].
5. Teaching the girls cooking, etc., whenever Mrs. Washington desires it in connection with [the girl students'] department. We shall go on as fast as we can in fitting up your research laboratory.[13]

In a follow-up letter, he added,

I fear that you . . . are inclined to misinterpret my suggestions which . . . in most cases, are but a polite way of giving orders. I do not want the Council to become a debating club, where every member feels that he must either object to or debate every order or suggestion given by the Principal. I have reasons for every order I give . . . and it is not necessary for any head to feel that when I do make suggestions that it is because he is not doing his duty or trying to do it.[14]

The last week of the year Carver resigned again, requesting

one month to "put my department in order, get my things packed, find storage for them, and incidentally get myself located."[15] He had been offered the position as head of either of two new experiment stations planned by the Department of Agriculture. Yet in the end, Professor Carver changed his mind once more and stayed put.

6

OUT OF THE SHADOW

In spite of his frustration, dissatisfaction, and continuing political battles, Carver never left Tuskegee. His threats to resign were less about science and teaching than about getting the praise and attention he thought he deserved. However willing the professor was momentarily to bolt for better conditions elsewhere in the wake of a disagreement with Washington or Bridgeforth, his deep loyalty to Tuskegee and devotion to his students always trumped. Though he still complained of broken promises and disrespect, by 1913, his seventeenth year at the school, Professor Carver had settled in for good.

Over those years, four areas had surfaced as Carver's principal interests. The professor didn't think of these as discrete, separate pursuits, but as interwoven disciplines he followed in whatever way circumstances, school responsibilities, and his own preferences led him. The first was classroom teaching. As much as Carver complained about it, he loved teaching and the students loved him. What he wanted to avoid was teaching in the academic department under George Bridgeforth or under any other conditions where he would have to answer administratively to someone else.

Second on his list of interests was his beloved laboratory. Years after leaving Iowa State for Tuskegee, Carver continued to insist he was promised better facilities and equipment than he had. Even so, he spent long hours working with the resources at hand and never seemed happier than when he was immersed in scientific study.

Third was commercial pursuits. A subtext in everything Carver did was that the results ought to help his students and the one-horse farmer achieve financial independence. The professor searched for commercial applications for his plant and crop research, and for other experiments he always had under way.

Fourth, and tying everything together, was his Christian witness that lifted up God as the Creator of all things, One who would reveal the secrets of creation to all who looked diligently and with a humble heart.

Professor Carver had been a natural in the classroom from the first, developing his teaching style the same way he approached science: intuitively, subjectively, guided by his own feelings instead of established norms. Time and again experience had proven his notion that young minds retained far more from exploring and discovering on their own than from rote lecture or reading a textbook. He taught about plants by using samples he'd collected on his early morning walks, leading field trips through the woods, and describing the beauty and perfection of a specimen in spiritual and artistic terms as well as scientific ones.

Having taught thousands of students by now, Professor Carver was as enthusiastic and compassionate as ever. He reached out to new students more as a friend than as a professor, asking them where they were from and learning about their families. Carver encouraged the newcomers and stayed in touch with them as the year progressed. He was a sympathetic sounding board for the catalog of problems—both real and imagined—that students carried to school with them. He was always ready with a kind word of encouragement or nugget of advice; despite his small size, he was known to play-wrestle with the boys on the ground.

After his students graduated or left the campus, Carver wrote to many of them, some for years afterward, following their careers, admonishing them to remember what they'd learned at school, and instructing them to be kind to others. Almost invariably his letters began, "My Dear Boy," and adopted a fatherly tone. For the three decades that followed, generations of students shared stories of Carver's kindness, teaching ability, generosity, and personal interest in them, and they treasured the letters he wrote by the hundreds.

As much as Professor Carver enjoyed and excelled at teaching, the center of his world was his laboratory, where he could pursue his lifelong interest in God's creation. As a small boy he had had his own garden where he examined and tended flowers, herbs, and other specimens; neighbors brought their sick plants to him when he was scarcely old enough to read. Later he coaxed a garden from the barren, windswept soil of western Kansas, and was known for nurturing a luxuriant "greenhouse" in a lean-to beside his employer's sod hut. With his art teacher Etta Budd encouraging him, he traded his painting studio for a botanical laboratory at Iowa State, taking advantage of a well equipped and fully supplied facility funded by a relatively generous state legislature.

The lack of what he considered a proper research lab had been one of his early disappointments at Tuskegee. For years the argument fell back into the same familiar track: Carver insisting he'd been promised a fully equipped lab as a condition of coming to Tuskegee instead of staying at Iowa for his doctorate, while Booker T. Washington and his administration believed it was unfair to the students to spend money on equipment and materials for one teacher's exclusive use. Carver finally began assembling the equipment he wanted, though it came slowly, much of it through scavenging.

For example, Carver chafed over the administration's request that he describe the glassware he needed and what each piece was for. To make do when the finance committee balked at his budget request, he made some equipment of his own. Salvaging an empty whiskey bottle in an alley, he tied a string around the center of it and immersed it in ice water. After the bottle was cold he set the string on fire, which cracked the bottle in half, making a funnel out of the top half and a beaker out of the bottom. It would be 1917 before Carver finally quit teaching altogether to devote all his time to laboratory experiments and research.

One justification Carver made for building and equipping a research lab was that it would eventually pay for itself in new discoveries and products. The professor remained keenly invested in developing and marketing profitable products made from simple natural ingredients. Carver often ran soil samples for companies and individuals to see how rich it was, what would grow best in it, and what kind of fertilizer or minerals it needed.

As early as 1902 he had identified a clay sample sent by the National Building and Loan Company of Montgomery, Alabama, as a potential source of valuable paint pigment. Combining his scientist's curiosity and his painter's eye, he produced a Prussian blue color that seemed at least equal to any other pigment available. Carver mixed batches of paint himself and tested them side by side. But when Carver sent samples to paint and pigment manufacturers, they pronounced them inferior to the pigments they were already using, adding that they had considered them only because they came from "Professor George W. Carver, the Chemist and Commissioner of Agriculture of the famous Tuskegee Normal and Industrial School [colored] of which Mr. Booker T. Washington is Principal."[1]

The prospect of commercial production resurfaced again in 1911, when Carver started working with some of his chemistry students to make whitewash, paint, and wood stain out of clay near the Tuskegee campus. The school began using these products on their buildings rather than buying paint; students painted their own dorm rooms with paint they had helped formulate.

A white Episcopal congregation in Tuskegee ordered Carver's stain for the interior of their new church building. They were elated with the results, at a price of one-tenth of what commercially manufactured stain would have cost. Carver reported the results in one of his continuing series of Experiment Station Bulletins. He also experimented with making dyes from a list of other plants including tomatoes, radishes, maple bark, and onions.

Carver also believed he could make a high-quality talcum powder from the same clay. Unfortunately the cosmetic application never got beyond the trial stage, and neither it nor the paint and stain business ever had any public promotion or retail distribution. In what would become a familiar pattern, Carver would develop a practical application with no idea how to reproduce or market it, and no one to help him. Finally he would abandon it to work on the next concept that captured his attention.

At one point Carver reported to the administration that the girls at Tuskegee could make fifty-three different products from poultry feathers that were now being thrown away. At the time Carver called it "the most valuable and astonishing" line of experimentation he'd ever undertaken, though again nothing came of it. He developed a new strain of cotton that promised large bolls and high disease resistance, but evidently never had the time or resources to promote it.

He continued in his efforts to make simple crops more versatile, believing that black-eyed peas, sweet potatoes, and peanuts showed the most promise. In an Experiment Station Bulletin of 1906, Carver listed a hundred and five recipes for peanuts, including a coffee substitute and peanut pie. To show-case his discoveries, he had some of the senior girls cook a complete meal for Washington, including the main dish and beverage, made of nothing but peanuts.

One of his food experiments yielded Carver an unanticipated personal benefit. After feeding Washington samples of meat he had preserved, Carver was delighted to hear Washington say they were excellent and that the school would stop buying canned meat and use his instead. To help with the slaughtering and preservation, Washington assigned Carver's nemesis and admin-istrative superior George Bridgeforth to assist. It was no surprise to Washington that Bridgeforth complained about having to work with Carver, which led the principal to write Bridgeforth in a memo, "The records in my office show that I spend more time in dealing with your Department and trying to get orders carried out . . . than I do with all the other departments combined."[2]

Binding all the threads of his life into one cord was Carver's overarching belief in a Creator who had made everything he studied so intently, and gave him and his students the insights to understand and appreciate them. Since Tuskegee students came from the Caribbean and Central America as well as the American South, there were generally non-Christians in his classes. Carver explained that the Creator God tied all creation and all learning together. As a student named Alvin D. Smith later explained, Carver told his students that his faith was

> the key to all that he had been able to do. Busy as he was with duties in his laboratory and botany circular classes, he did not

have [time] to add a Bible class. But knowing the background from which students of the rural South, Africa, and other lands came, he was anxious that they have this key, without which they could not unlock the kingdom of good things they desired, or that they deserved, regardless of race, color, or creed . . .

[With Carver's Bible lessons,] one is assured good out of every situation.[3]

Smith leaves a vivid picture of Carver the first night Smith attended his Bible class. Carver arrived in mismatched, wrinkled clothes with only the top coat button fastened, so that the rest of the coat splayed out. He had a fresh poppy blossom in his lapel. Carver taught Bible class without a Bible; he didn't read from one or even refer to it directly. In a surprisingly high-pitched tone, Carver started to speak, but the boys soon forgot about the strange sounding voice as they sensed his warmth and kindness. Carver began:

Your faces are beaming with happiness tonight. Your lives will be filled with happiness if you contact thy Creator and keep tuned in with him.

Each of you came to Tuskegee to learn a trade, to study the academic courses and graduate and then go out into the world. You are enthusiastic about that now, but if you do not know how to turn the key to the storehouse of happiness— how to contact and keep tuned in with our Creator—you are in for many unhappy situations.

The advice of Solomon can come in handy here. With all thy getting, get understanding—understanding that our Creator is Law and he will give us the happiness our hearts desire, if we follow his Laws.[4]

Several lessons later, a group of students asked the professor to explain exactly what the Creator was. Carver began his answer by quoting John 4:24 from memory:

"God is a Spirit, and they that worship him must worship him in spirit and in truth." To refer to him as God or to call him our Creator is one and the same.

Our Creator, being Spirit, is Principle—Law and by keeping his laws, we get from him good, for he is good. The things we go to our Creator for must be good things; he has nothing else to give us and through us for the benefit of mankind—regardless of race except good. Persons who attempt to contact him with a selfish and mean motive in mind are defeated before they start and are driven from the temple to failure.[5]

That led to another student's question: If God were a Spirit, did that mean they would never be able to see him?

Carver pointed to the flower in his lapel. "When you look at this flower, you see thy Creator. Students at Tuskegee who are studying to be electricians are not able to see electricity, but when they make the proper contact—fulfill the laws of their trade—a bulb lights the way, not only for them, but for all of us."[6]

Busy and popular with the students as Professor Carver was, his star shown brightly in a relatively narrow world. He was almost unknown outside Tuskegee and the scientific community after nineteen years on the faculty. His teaching, Bible study, agricultural bulletins, fairs, Jessup Wagon work, demonstrations, and displays were concentrated in a small area in rural Alabama. His bulletins, which found their way to rural farmers around the world, and occasional magazine articles gave a larger audience only a glimpse of this innovative Negro scientist and educator.

Booker T. Washington had mentioned Carver a few times to a national audience, once notably in his *Atlantic Monthly* article of 1903, where he held up the professor as an example of "how far above the horizon of the average individual one is permitted to rise, and how far into the future he is permitted to see, a sort of horoscope of God to foresee and work out the destiny of a great race of people."[7]

He added, "I have always said that the best means . . . for destroying race prejudice is to make [oneself] a useful, and if possible, an indispensable member of the community in which he lives. I do not know of a better illustration of this than may be found in the case of Professor Carver."[8] In his 1911 book, *My Larger Education*, Washington repeated the praise lavished on Carver by Sir Harry Johnson during his visit to Tuskegee the year before, and added compliments of his own.

Carver's old friend James Wilson cited him in an interview with *Technical World Magazine*, highlighting Carver's early artistic promise and his devotion to his people. When

Wilson and other scientific peers sent complimentary letters, Carver forwarded them to Washington to make sure he knew how much his professional colleagues held him in esteem. Years of frustration over not getting the attention he thought he deserved at school made him all the more hungry for accolades from elsewhere.

During the years Professor Carver toiled in relative obscurity at Tuskegee, Booker T. Washington became the most renowned black man in America and arguably the most famous black individual in the world. He burst onto the national scene during the Cotton States Exposition of 1895 in Atlanta, where he spoke at the opening ceremonies. He encouraged his audience to accept the black race as equals in business and under law, while assuring them that the "wisest" of his race "understand that the agitation of questions of social equality is in the extremest folly, and that progress in the enjoyment of all the privileges that will come to us must be the result of severe and constant struggle rather than of artificial forcing."

A standing-room-only crowd estimated at fifteen thousand roared its approval in a "delerium of applause." The Atlanta *Constitution* reported that the speech "could not have been excelled." The New York *World* heralded Washington as a "Negro Moses." President Grover Cleveland telegrammed his congratulations, saying that reaction to Washington's speech "cannot fail to delight and encourage all who wish well for your race."[9]

In 1899, fearful that their principal was working himself to death, wealthy Northern trustees and benefactors of Tuskegee sent Washington and his wife on a three-month European vacation. Though he repeatedly declined invitations to speak, he addressed the University Club of Paris, where he met former president Benjamin Harrison, and the American Embassy in London, where he met members of Parliament along with Mark Twain, who was also visiting. Washington accepted an invitation to Windsor Castle, where he was presented to Queen Victoria.

In 1911 Washington was assaulted in a New York apartment building, requiring sixteen stitches to close wounds in his head and ear. By that time he had already undergone treatment for severe indigestion at a popular and exclusive sanitarium in Michigan run by the Kellogg family. He also underwent a complete medical workover at St. Mary's Hospital in Rochester, Minnesota, where Drs. William and Charles Mayo had opened a clinic. By 1915 he was buying stomach pills by the hundreds, had kidney stones, and registered blood pressure of 215. Refusing to slow down, he continued traveling, speaking, and meeting with school benefactors at his usual breakneck pace.

On November 5, 1915, Washington was admitted to a New York hospital with what the *Tribune* described as "a nervous breakdown." The patient believed his end was near, and insisted on going home to die. "I was born in the South," he said. "I have lived in the South, and I expect to die and be buried in the South." The afternoon of November 12, leaning heavily on his petite wife's arm, he boarded the train for home. Arriving at Chechaw, the station nearest Tuskegee, the next night,

Washington fell asleep in the ambulance on the drive home and died the following morning in his own bed.[10]

George Washington Carver was shattered by Washington's death to the extent that he was unable to teach for a while and was reassigned to monitor a study hall. When the school organized a memorial fund in Washington's honor, Carver donated a thousand dollars—a year's salary. The acting principal, Emmett Scott, thanked Carver for his generous donation and commented that such a large gift required great sacrifice.

"True it is," Carver answered. "It was a sacrifice in one way but a blessed privilege in another. I am sure Mr. Washington never knew how much I loved him, and the cause for which he gave his life."[11]

As long as Washington was alive Carver always stood in his gigantic shadow. Washington wrote the books, hobnobbed with presidents, moved comfortably in circles with America's richest industrialists and businessmen, and took tea with the queen at Windsor Castle. Washington was a powerful presence, articulate, immaculately dressed, always ramrod straight whether sitting, riding, or standing, and a gifted orator and writer. Carver remained in his classroom, his laboratory, and his woods, nurturing his plants and the young minds that came to him for guidance. When Washington died, the stage was set for Carver to emerge from the shadows and blossom in the sun like one of his experiments.

In the spring of May 1915, shortly before Washington's death, Carver received a gift of $125 in honor of his "valued service" from Julius Rosenwald, president of Sears, Roebuck and Company and a key financial supporter of Tuskegee. It was one of the few recorded acknowledgments of Carver's contributions up to that time. A year later, a columnist wrote Tuskegee asking for an appointment with a "Mr. Carter. I am not absolutely clear about Mr. Carter but it seems to me he has made distinguished contributions to the race."[12]

That same year, 1916, Carver's reputation began to gather critical mass. The Baltimore *Afro-American* newspaper reported the professor's belief that ability and results mattered more than race. Carver's theory was that whoever could "produce the most milk, make the best butter, raise the finest and cheapest beef, pork, mutton, fowl, etc., put upon the market superior fruits, grains, and in short gilt edge products of every kind, and at the least expense and the least injury to the soil, will be in constant demand, regardless to the color of his skin or the texture of his hair."[13]

More important, the mainstream white establishment was paying new attention to Carver. The year the *Afro-American* article appeared, Carver accepted an invitation to join the advisory board of the National Agricultural Society and was elected a Fellow of the Royal Society for the Encouragement of Arts, Manufactures, and Commerce in London.

Impressive as they were, these honors were still limited to the scientific field. Carver's first taste of sustained popular attention came after America entered World War I in April 1917. With overseas trade suddenly halted, the United States had to find substitutes for common items or do without them. George Washington Carver was filled to overflowing with ideas about how to substitute homegrown raw materials for formerly imported goods. He said he was working on making rubber from sweet potatoes and rope from peanut hulls. The best pigments, many of which came from Germany, could be replaced by substitutes made of local clay or native plants. In interviews, Carver assured America that bread flour to feed its soldiers could come from sweet potatoes as well.

Newspaper photos of this curious-looking man showed a small black figure in a rumpled lab coat decorated with a fresh flower and standing in a gleaming laboratory—Carver had his long-promised lab at last. His mustache and hair were gray and he stooped as he walked. Yet his eyes shone with the excitement of discovery. As he appeared more often in the press, Carver was described as a "chemist" or "research scientist," though his entire professional career and training was as a botanist. About this time or soon afterward, people began referring to him as "Dr. Carver." Though he never earned his doctorate, Carver never corrected the misnomer, and happily accepted the informal, honorific title. Within a few years he would be universally known as Dr. Carver.

After the Allied victory in 1918, America found itself emerging as a center of economic power and heavily invested in overseas trade. As the national standard of living rose, it became harder for domestic farmers to compete in the marketplace. Overseas growers could produce goods cheaper than their American counterparts; the Americans ran the risk of being priced out of business. To protect the domestic farm economy, growers and traders lobbied Congress for protective tariffs on a variety of foods. One lobbying group, appearing in a mundane hearing before the House Ways and Means Committee, inadvertently completed the transformation of George Washington Carver from obscure botany professor to international celebrity.

SCIENCE SHALL MAKE
YOU FREE

The United Peanut Growers Association mounted a full-court press in Congress to protect its members from the economic consequences of competition from cheap imports. A bill in the House of Representatives looked promising, proposing a substantial import duty on peanuts, but its progress was slow and tenuous. The process began in a House committee that held hearings, then voted the bill up or down. If it was approved, it passed "out of committee" to the full House for debate and final voting. Committee hearings could take weeks or months before a bill made it to the House floor, if it made it at all.

As a trade-related bill, the peanut tariff legislation originated in the House Ways and Means Committee. Day after day, Representatives assembled in their ornate, high-ceilinged committee room on Capitol Hill to listen to a parade of witnesses explain why the farmers they represented needed trade protection from foreign growers. Each witness was allowed ten minutes.

On January 20, 1921, chairman Joseph W. Fordney, a Republican from Michigan, gaveled the Ways and Means Committee to order for another day of testimony on the importance of domestic peanuts to the American economy, which promised to be much like the day before, and the day before that. That assumption changed when the next witness was called and a nattily dressed black man, graying, thin, and slightly stooped, entered the large, elegant room with a big box under his arm. He was introduced to the committee as George Washington Carver, from Tuskegee Institute in Alabama. Chairman Fordney reminded the witness that he had ten minutes and invited him to proceed.

United Peanut Growers knew Carver by reputation and had retained him as an expert on peanuts. Outside the South and outside the study of agriculture, no one had any notion who he was. Very likely not a single member of the committee had ever heard Carver's name. The small black man settled himself in his seat at the witness table and asked if he could make room for some of the exhibits he had brought. Decades of teaching had shown him the power of not only saying what he had to say, but also demonstrating it in a memorable way. As the previously bored committee members leaned forward in their chairs, Professor Carver began unpacking his box. He set out blocks of crushed peanut meats that he called "crushed cake," explaining that it made a tasty breakfast cereal and many other products he didn't have time to list in ten minutes.[1] He showed the committee ground peanut hulls, which he said were good for burnishing tin.

The chairman asked slyly if Carver had brought anything to drink—a reference to Prohibition, which had been in effect a little more than a year. When Carver answered that liquid examples might "come later if my ten minutes are extended," the committee broke out in laughter that continued until Fordney rapped his gavel for order. The professor showed his audience chocolate covered peanuts and a sample of breakfast food made from peanuts and sweet potatoes. "I am very sorry that you can not taste this, so I will taste it for you," he said, taking a bite. Once more the committee rippled with laughter.

Peanuts and sweet potatoes, Carver explained, were "two of the greatest products that God has ever given us." If every other vegetable on earth was destroyed, Carver testified, "a perfectly balanced ration with all of the nutrients in it could be made with the sweet potato and the peanut. From the sweet potato we get starches and carbohydrates, and from the peanut we get all the muscle-building properties."

Here one of the committee members interrupted the witness. John Q. Tilson, Republican from Connecticut, asked, "Do you want a watermelon to go along with that?"

A grinning colored man eating a watermelon—and showing lots of white teeth—was a stereotypical image of the time. Carver didn't miss a beat. "Of course, if you want a dessert, that comes in very well, but you know we can get along pretty well without dessert."

Every minute or two Carver reached into what he called his "Pandora's box" to pull out another example: peanut bars held in shape with sweet potato syrup, peanut hay for livestock, dyes, a quinine substitute. When his ten minutes were up, Chairman Fordney offered him more time.

Pressed about specifics of a proposed tariff, Carver wisely deferred. He was there to talk about peanuts, not about the law, and would leave the legal argument to the Growers Association. But he added, "I wish to say here in all sincerity that America produces better peanuts than any part of the world, as far as I have been able to test them out."

The Ways and Means Committee segued into talk of other food substitutes. John Nance Garner, a Democrat from Texas who would later be FDR's vice president, commented that the dairy lobby had been trying to convince the committee to tax oleomargarine "to put it out of business."

"Oh yes," Carver agreed enthusiastically. "Yes, sir. That's all the tariff means—to put the other fellow out of business." Startled and amused by such innocent candor, the committee laughed louder than ever, the sound echoing off the high marble walls. Members added to the noise with a round of applause.

When the commotion died down enough for him to be heard, Chairman Fordney said to the smiling professor, "Go ahead, brother. Your time is unlimited."

Carver moved on to discuss peanut milk, which he displayed beside a bottle of cow's milk. The two looked almost identical, complete with "cream" floating on top. He said peanut milk could be used to make buttermilk, instant coffee,

Worcestershire sauce, cheese, salad oil, ink, fruit punch, and much more.

He closed his testimony by saying that peanuts were part of a "natural diet" given as a great gift from the Creator.

> If you go to the first chapter of Genesis, we can interpret very clearly, I think, what God intended when he said, "Behold, I have given you every herb that bears seed upon the face of the earth, and every tree bearing a seed. To you it shall be meat." That is what he means about it. "It shall be meat." There is everything there to strengthen and nourish and keep the body alive and healthy.

Again the committee applauded warmly. Carver explained that everything he showed them had come from his research laboratory at Tuskegee. He'd found 107 uses for the sweet potato but was just starting on the peanut. There was no telling how many applications for the peanut he would eventually discover, but, he said, his demonstration before the committee represented about half of what he had so far.

Representative Allen Treadway, a Republican from Massachusetts, replied, "Well, come again and bring the rest." Professor Carver had held the jaded politicians of the House Ways and Means Committee spellbound for an hour and forty minutes.

Eventually the committee approved the highest tariff ever on peanuts up to that time, three cents a pound shelled and four cents unshelled.

Carver's appearance was a rare event in that it showed the public an intelligent, articulate black person who made an important contribution to all society, including white society. Blacks were generally considered prone to laziness, uneducated, untrustworthy, slow-witted, and thought of mostly as janitors, railroad porters, dishwashers, and other menial workers. Yet here was a professor, a scientist, a recognized expert with a graduate degree, teaching congressmen in Washington what they needed to know to consider national legislation. Playing against the popular stereotype, he was courteous, well mannered, the polar opposite of the unwashed, chicken-stealing rural rubes much of white society assumed all black people to be. In this gentle educator there was no hint of a threat or of racial discord.

Like Booker T. Washington, Professor Carver held his tongue in the face of the racial slurs and discrimination that were part of his everyday life. With very few exceptions across the nation, black customers were not allowed in restaurants or hotels that served whites; an owner might sell them a sandwich at the kitchen door as long as white diners didn't notice. If a theater let them in, it was to sit in the "colored balcony." Some churches had separate balconies that black and white alike called "nigger heaven." Seating was segregated at sporting events, speaking engagements, and other public gatherings. Railroad and bus stations had separate colored waiting rooms. Black train passengers rode in designated cars only. Public rest rooms and water fountains were strictly for whites; sometimes there were separate facilities for colored and sometimes not. If there weren't, blacks did without. Help wanted ads were categorized by "Help Wanted—White" and "Help Wanted—Colored," with the latter being mostly yard men and street sweepers. In the rare cases when blacks made headway in a trade—masons and blacksmiths were two that had a relatively high concentration of black workers—black wages were lower than white.

Prominent blacks had criticized Booker T. Washington for being too passive and accommodating in the face of institutional discrimination. W. E. B. Du Bois, a Harvard PhD and college professor who became a renowned proponent of black resistance; John Hope, president of Atlanta Baptist College; and Francis James Grimké, a prominent Washington DC pastor, were among those high profile black leaders who insisted patience and forbearance had failed and it was time to fight for equal civil rights.

After Washington's death and Carver's appearance before the House committee, Carver became the new public face in support of persuasion by humility, selflessness, and excellence that blacks deserved humane and respectful treatment. Like Washington, Carver made it clear that he wasn't looking for social interaction with whites, but for equal opportunity in jobs, education, public accommodation, and other practical areas. Carver didn't fight for his rights; rather he proved through patient example that he—and by extension, all blacks everywhere—was worthy of them.

For more than a year after his Ways and Means Committee appearance, Carver saw his story retold time and again in newspapers across the country. The tale of a slave boy kidnapped by marauders and raised by his former owners made tremendous copy. He was a personal friend of the current secretary of agriculture, former Iowa professor Henry C. Wallace. He was a lovable eccentric who wore mismatched clothes in the lab and forgot to deposit his paychecks until the business office at Tuskegee reminded him. His life was "a tragedy and a romance," one writer declared. Articles often pointed out the broad potential of his work. Another observer wrote, "His service has been to no class, but to the nation."

Booker T. Washington was once called "the Wizard of Tuskegee."[2] After Washington's accomplishments began receding into history, that mantle fell upon Carver's frail shoulders. The press acclaimed Carver as a "great specialist in foods and food values," and the "wizard chemist." As he had since his days as a homesteader in western Kansas, Carver encouraged a sense of mystery about his life story and left impressive-sounding mistakes uncorrected. In 1922, shortly after Carver's official retirement from Tuskegee, the alumni listed him as a retired professor of chemistry rather than his official, though less impressive sounding, title as director of agriculture.

One of the most intriguing and longest running mysteries about Carver was that during World War I, Thomas Edison had offered him a job at his research laboratory in New Jersey. As early as 1917 Carver admitted he'd been recruited but that "there was nothing to talk over, and I thanked Mr. Edison in a letter." True to form, Carver evidently turned down a far better financial arrangement elsewhere to stay with his work and "his people" at Tuskegee.

How much better the arrangement was remains the big mystery. Supposedly an associate of Edison's named Hutchinson carried the offer to Carver in person at Tuskegee; Edison was busy redesigning the electrical system for America's submarine fleet. From the time he came to Tuskegee in 1896 until Washington's death in 1915, Carver's salary remained a thousand dollars a year. Edison's offer was rumored to be a hundred thousand dollars a year. Some reports put it at two hundred thousand, others at "five times the salary of the President of the United States," whose annual salary then was seventy-five thousand dollars (equal to about 1.7 million dollars in modern purchasing power when it was set in 1909). Carver repeatedly declined requests to reveal how much Edison actually offered, even as he kept the mystery alive by mentioning it in interviews.[3]

Tuskegee delighted in the new wave of publicity Carver and his peanut testimony brought to the school. Robert Russa Moton, a graduate of Hampton Institute, Washington's alma mater, and an administrator there before coming to Tuskegee, succeeded Washington as head of the school. Moton complimented Carver's "modest, unassuming manner" and saw him as a public relations gold mine, where Washington had invariably seen a gifted but high-maintenance teacher and researcher.

The news media continued their praise, anointing Carver as the "Columbus of the Soil," "God's Ebony Scientist," and "a colored Horatio Alger." A steady stream of visitors from across the country traveled to Alabama to call on this amazing little man. If they came upon him collecting botany samples on campus or at the side of the road, strangers were likely to mistake him for the gardener or an old man wandering aimlessly through the neighborhood. By the mid-1920s he was in constant demand as a speaker. He accepted some of the invitations, but was never happier than when in his laboratory seeing what miracles God revealed. "I didn't make these discoveries," he insisted. "God has only worked through me to reveal to his children some of his wonderful providence."[4]

The fact that Carver had no interest whatsoever in profiting personally from his discoveries made him even more endearing to his growing list of admirers and the public at large. As a Tuskegee alumni publication once reported:

> He does not expect to withhold from the world the benefit of his remarkable discoveries, but he declares that when they are commercialized, his race shall receive full credit for them. He is almost daily turning down offers to market his products with the Negro racial identity eliminated . . . The invention of the automobile, the cotton gin, spindle and loom will have no greater importance than Professor Carver's discoveries.[5]

A feature in *Success* magazine affirmed the professor's perspective in his work on pigments:

> The magic colors which adorned the works of art in Tutankhamen's tomb and stand resplendent and unfaded after thirty centuries, an art lost to modern workers in

pigments, this magician has produced in cold water paints compounded from the clays he has dug out of the hills and pits of the South.[6]

While he basked in the adulation, the professor also held fast to his belief that his results were the product of God's bounty and love rather than any skill or ability on his part. And always, always, he was striving first of all to lift the spirits and the fortunes of blacks everywhere.

"They say that science is classified knowledge," Carver explained. "I know that science is truth. Jesus said, 'Ye shall know the Truth and the Truth will set you free.' It seems to me that he meant, 'You shall know science and science shall make you free.' "[7]

SIMPLY THE TRUTH

Professor Carver's thin-skinned personality was a liability and a constant source of friction during the Booker T. Washington years at Tuskegee. As Carver became more of a public figure, that same sensitivity made him all the more endearing. It also helped sustain Carver's popularity on campus even after he retired from teaching. Though he no longer instructed in the classroom, Carver maintained an unflagging level of personal interest in students. The life lessons and religious guidance he gave them informally proved far more long lasting and valuable than whatever they might have learned about botany. Many had never had a strong parental figure in their lives. In turn, Carver had no relations of his own, and the students were the only family he had.

When former students wrote for advice, the professor encouraged them with admonitions to work hard, deal humbly with adversaries, and trust in God to see them through. To one student who poured his heart out in a letter, Carver replied:

You are now in the midst of a great struggle. You are fighting for freedom, you will win, God is on your side . . . My friend I love you for what you are and what you hope to be through Jesus Christ.

There are times when I am surely tried and am compelled to hide away with Jesus for strength to overcome. God alone knows what I have suffered, in trying to do as best I could the job he has given me in trust to do, most of the time I had to work without the sympathy or support of those with whom I associated. Many are the strange paths God led me into. He is and will lead you likewise.[1]

The professor was especially pleased to hear from students who left Tuskegee to start schools of their own. These institutions were usually poorly organized, poorly funded, and most of them lasted only a few years. Nonetheless, they brought Professor Carver's teaching, enthusiasm, and encouragement to another circle of eager, hard-working young black men and women who would never have had it otherwise. H. B. Bennett, a student of Carver's, wrote with excitement about the school he had founded on the professor's model in the rural hamlet of Stallo, Mississippi:

If you had any idea what you have done in this community through me, I am sure you could die happy. Think of a community five years ago in its way to the Promised Land. Its humble servant, your son, is so very happy because of the change.

Prof., the reason I give you credit for what little I have tried to do, is because it was you who laid the right foundation for my life's journey. I can look back and see how I would have failed time and again had it not been for your good instruction.

Bennett proudly added that he had relied on Carver's example to deal with personal conflicts as well as academic challenges. He told the story of a man he said was "bitterly opposed" to him, and how he applied Carver's tools of patience and Christian witness.

I never retaliated one bit; I used righteousness, patience, and self-control, and won out . . . He comes to my house now, sits down and talks about how to get through life. He is a completely converted man . . . This little verse comes to me now, from the Bible: "The righteous shall never be moved." Now, this is not my victory; it is yours; because, had you not impressed my whole life, I am sure I would have retaliated.[2]

For Christmas 1921 the senior class at Tuskegee gave the professor a fountain pen. Writing to thank the class president, Carver made a point of reinforcing the attributes he considered essential. These, to Carver, remained far more important than anything students might learn in the classroom. True to form, he considered himself their "father" and referred to them as his "children."

As your father, it is needless for me to keep saying, I hope, except for emphasis, that each one of my children will rise to the full height of your possibilities, which means the possession of these eight cardinal virtues which constitutes a lady or a gentleman.

1st. Be clean both inside and outside.

2nd. Who neither looks up to the rich or down on the poor.

3rd. Who loses, if need be, without squealing.

4th. Who wins without bragging.

5th. Who is always considerate of women, children, and old people.

6th. Who is too brave to lie.

7th. Who is too generous to cheat.

8th. Who takes his share of the world and lets other people have theirs.[3]

In keeping with his advice to students, Carver remained quietly on the sidelines as public debate over race relations grew in the wake of the World War. He was content to serve as an example of black achievement rather than as its spokesman. Even so, Carver's public profile grew throughout the 1920s. He found himself applauded not only by those who, like Washington, counseled patience and advised against confronting institutionalized discrimination head-on, but also by those who had despised Washington because they thought he was too passive and too close to his influential white friends with names like Carnegie and Roosevelt. Because Carver represented no threat or opposition to them the way Washington had as a writer, lecturer, and school president, the more confrontational blacks traded on his popularity and spoke well of him in the press.

Some of Washington's harshest critics had formed the National Association for the Advancement of Colored People, in part to challenge the power of what they called the "Tuskegee Machine": Washington's influential network of connections—some public, others private—with politicians, industrialists, opinion leaders, and key editors of both the white and black press, which promoted his viewpoint on racial reform and muffled the opposition. It was a measure both of Carver's appeal to all sides of the race debate and of the fact they saw him as nothing of a threat, that in 1923 the NAACP presented to the professor their ultimate stamp of honor and approval.

Each year the organization awarded the Spingarn Medal—named for Joel Spingarn, a white publisher and one of the group's first chairmen—to "the man or woman of African descent and American citizenship who during the year shall have made the highest achievement in any field of human endeavor." The award was given to Professor Carver, according to the accompanying citation, for his research into uses for the peanut (he had ultimately found 145) and the sweet potato (107). While admitting many of these uses would never be commercially practical, "they indicate radical genius devoted to practical ends which men of all races must admire."[4]

Legal, political, and social relations between black and white had seemed on the verge of transformation after the Civil War. Yet in the wake of Reconstruction, states passed their own laws that effectively locked free blacks in as second-class citizens. By the time Carver received his accolade from the NAACP, the racial landscape of America had been transformed to such an extent that Booker T. Washington would scarcely have recognized it. Until the United States entered the Great War in 1917, the "race issue," as segregation was known, was largely academic outside of the old Cotton South.

The vast majority of African Americans were descendants of slaves and had no reason to move away from the Southern towns where they had lived for generations. (One noteworthy exception was Washington DC, where many blacks moved for government jobs in an atmosphere of relatively benign discrimination laws. The District of Columbia was a haven from the patchwork quilt of state laws that effectively neutralized the so-called Reconstruction Amendments XIII, XIV, and XV outlawing slavery, guaranteeing citizenship, and guaranteeing the right to vote.)

Four and a half million soldiers, almost all white, served in World War I, leaving four and a half million civilian jobs unfilled. Under different circumstances, foreign workers would likely have stepped in to take their places, but the war in Europe had shut off the flow of immigrants. Desperate factory owners sent agents south to offer blacks free train tickets to Chicago, Detroit, and other industrial centers to man the machines and assembly lines. Seeing a once-in-a-lifetime opportunity to better themselves, blacks by the tens of thousands left their hardscrabble farms and subsistence wages for the promise of job training and regular paychecks in the North.

So many fortune seekers pulled up stakes that in some towns the railroad refused to sell tickets to black migrants. Blacks heard rumors that they would freeze in the unfamiliar cold. And yet they went.

In the spring of 1919 the victorious American doughboys returned to a hero's welcome—and expected their old jobs back. Black workers who had gambled everything on a future in the industrial North were summarily fired or demoted to menial work. Many of them couldn't afford a ticket home and wouldn't have wanted to go back to farming even if they had the fare. Black families were herded into slums, competing against returning white soldiers both for space and for suddenly scarce employment. Whites felt invaded; blacks felt betrayed.

Race riots flared in one city after another, some causing monumental damage, all tearing at America's social fabric. In Chicago that year a black boy drowned in Lake Michigan after his raft drifted to a white beach and white boys threw rocks at it. That tragic death brought calls for retribution, inciting neighbor to war against neighbor. It took the state militia two days to reclaim the streets. By then, thirty-eight people were dead and more than five hundred injured. In Tulsa two years later, a black shoeshine boy may have tripped entering an elevator, reflexively grabbing the arm of the white female elevator operator to break his fall. The boy was arrested, a lynch mob formed, and by the time the national guard arrived, thirty-nine rioters had died, eight hundred were injured, and thirty-five city blocks were in flames. In 1923 the town of Rosewood, Florida, was completely destroyed and abandoned following riots after a black drifter was accused of assaulting a white woman in her home.

Against this background of violence, it was gentle, nonconfrontational, articulate, and accomplished George Washington Carver who demonstrated to American society how blacks and whites could respect each other, learn from each other, and how they needed each other. Commentators pointed out time and again that the professor's discoveries helped white and black alike. It seemed the more that was written about him, the more people wanted to write. An editorial in the *St. Louis Globe Democrat* for March 28, 1923, began, "There is the interest which surrounds occurrences high extraordinary in an account stating that a Negro born in Missouri as a slave, has been made a Fellow of the royal Society of Great Britain . . . He is honored by British scientists for having made a number of very remarkable chemical discoveries . . ."[5]

Newspapers across the country hailed him as "a man of international repute," "acceded to be one of the world's greatest scientists," "a genius who lives in closest touch with nature," "a wizard of organic chemistry." Some of his more enthusiastic boosters declared Professor Carver would add a hundred million dollars a year to the wealth of the South. When he was at Tuskegee, Carver continued with laboratory research and botanical studies as he had for decades, now in a facility equipped with everything he wanted. The school recognized Carver's inestimable value to their image and, in contrast to the Washington years, went out of their way to make him comfortable. He spent increasingly more time on the road speaking about the peanut, the sweet potato, and his views of God in nature, complete with the demonstrations that had so entranced the Ways and Means Committee. Reporting on the professor's lecture at the Cecil Hotel in Atlanta, the *Atlanta Constitution* declared, "The Scripture was literally fulfilled: 'See thou a man diligent in business, he shall stand before kings.'"[6]

Even the United Daughters of the Confederacy, staunch defenders of the romanticized ideal of the Southern cause, sent the professor a resolution passed during an exhibit of his work in Atlanta in 1923, "a written expression of their interest and appreciation of you in your efforts to exhibit the products and possible industries of our South, and the Chapter wishes you God-Speed in any endeavor looking to the development of any project in which we are naturally interested."[7]

These are remarkable words to a man born a slave from an organization carrying the standard of traditional Southern aristocracy. They underscore the respect Carver received from every walk of society. Yet for all the honors lavished on him, he could still be denied a seat on a train, a table at a restaurant, or permission to use a restroom because of his race. Carver never complained about these laws or tested them; rather he patiently labored to demonstrate he was the white man's equal and worthy of equal treatment.

Professor Carver's approach to scientific inquiry was unusual in that it skirted the scientific method. This is the accepted standard of experimentation that begins with a thesis or tentative conclusion based on existing knowledge, then uses carefully documented steps anyone can repeat to prove or disprove the new thesis. Experimental steps are performed time and again with a single controlled change each time—a varying amount of one fertilizer ingredient, for example, or growing identical plant samples at different temperatures.

This is the empirical, rational, logical process scientists generally use in their research. Carver had always been intuitive and subjective in his methods. In his public lectures, as he had done in class, Carver explained that God the Creator revealed the miracles of his creation to anybody willing to look for them. God's nature was a great gift, ours for the taking if we would only accept it. From the time he developed this unorthodox professional perspective, no one had ever questioned it on the grounds that it was inadequate science, overly dependent on intuition and puttering around the lab at the expense of careful analysis and documentation. As Carver became a national figure, his methods became subject to greater scrutiny and higher standards of proof.

In November 1924 Carver spoke at the landmark Marble Collegiate Church on Fifth Avenue in New York. There he repeated his belief that scientific discoveries were a product of divine revelation, not the scientific method. He looked for God's keys to the mysteries of the universe and evidently had no interest in acquiring a base of known facts to build upon. Students had commented in past years that the professor taught a Bible study without using a Bible. To his audience at Marble Collegiate Church he said that "no books ever go into my laboratory."[8]

"I never have to grope for methods," he continued. "The

method is revealed at the moment I am inspired to create something new."

A reporter with the *New York Times* challenged Carver's position. Two days after his speech, on November 20, the paper ran an editorial titled "Men of Science Never Talk That Way," declaring the professor displayed a "complete lack of scientific spirit" that reflected poorly on him, his race, and Tuskegee. Bona fide researchers in Carver's field "do not scorn books out of which they can learn what other chemists have done, and they do not ascribe their successes, when they have any, to 'inspiration.'"[9]

The *Times* was inundated with letters supporting Carver and criticizing their editorial stance. Other advocates wrote encouragement to Carver, and sent him copies of their letters to the *Times*. The professor said he was relieved at the public support, not for his own personal vindication but because the editorial had criticized Christianity. Prominent among the bulging mailbags was a letter to the editor from Carver himself. As often happened when he was agitated, Carver wrote in a somewhat scattered and nonlinear style (just as he so frequently conducted his experiments). His statement to the contrary notwithstanding, between the lines he clearly took offense at having his scholarship and credentials questioned. His reply leaves behind one of the most detailed explanations in his own words of his approach to science.

I regret exceedingly that such a gross misunderstanding should arise as to what is meant by "Divine inspiration."

Inspiration is never at variance with information; in fact, the more information one has, the greater will be the inspiration.

Paul, the great Scholar, says, Second Timothy 2:15, "Study to show thyself approved unto God, a Workman that needeth not to be ashamed, rightly dividing the word of truth."

Again he says in Galatians 1:12: "For I neither received it of man, neither was I taught it, but by the revelation of Jesus Christ . . ."

I receive the leading scientific publications. I thoroughly understand that there are scientists to whom the world is merely the result of chemical forces or material electrons. I do not belong to this class . . . The master analyst needs no book . . .

An Example: While in your beautiful city, I was struck with the large number of Taros and Yautias [vegetables typically grown in tropical climates] displayed in many of your markets; they are edible roots imported to this country. Just as soon as I saw them, I marveled at the wonderful possibilities for their expansion. Dozens of things came to me while standing there looking at them. I would follow the same or similar lines I have pursued in developing products from the white potato. I know of no one who has ever worked with these roots in this way. I know of no book from which I can get this information, yet I will have no trouble in doing it.

If this is not inspiration and information from a source greater than myself, or greater than any one has wrought up to the present time, kindly tell me what it is.

"And ye shall know the truth and the truth shall make you free." John 8:32.

Science is simply the truth about anything.[10]

Carver wrote very little for the public eye; nearly all of what has survived is in private letters to friends and students. Here he has left a rare and valuable window into his worldview and his notion of the essential connection between faith and science. Once the episode died down, Carver saw it in perspective as a life lesson from God. "After all," he reminded himself, "God moves in a mysterious way His wonders to perform."

Summarizing his position in a letter to a former student, he concluded:

As soon as you begin to read the great and loving God out of all forms of existence he has created, both animate and inanimate, then you will be able to Converse with him, anywhere, everywhere, and at all times. Oh, what a fullness of joy will come to you. My dear friend, get the significance. God is speaking.[11]

THE PEANUT MAN

By the mid-1920s George Washington Carver was a national celebrity. Notoriety did nothing to alter his character. There was still the winsome combination of childishness and experience, the kind demeanor, the self-effacing public humility that somewhat obscured an unflagging love of attention and praise. Millions knew him as the white-haired, soft-spoken colored scientist who had done so much for his race and for the betterment of farmers everywhere. Carver used his powerful name recognition to nurture promising commercial opportunities and then, in theory, used them to generate funds to support more research.

Earlier business ventures, including his paint and pigment business, had failed because the products were too expensive to market or there were already suitable versions of them available. In 1925, the animal feed and cereal manufacturing giant Ralston-Purina approached Professor Carver about developing a new breakfast cereal for them. Carver declined the offer, but it renewed his interest in commercializing his inventions. The professor warmed to the idea of heading his own company in order to develop marketable products with his unique scientific approach.

A wealthy white Tuskegee man, Ernest Thompson, had long been an admirer of Carver and had given him money and equipment over the years for research and experiments. The two of them shared a vision for a nonprofit company that would identify worthwhile products, refine them for commercial applications, then manufacture and market them at rock-bottom prices. They called their enterprise the Carver Products Company, and invited prospective investors to Tuskegee with the hope they would fund the business. To their disappointment, they learned that their most enthusiastic supporters were the least likely to have any investment capital. Other prospective partners had plenty of resources and business acumen. They were the skeptical ones, however, who wanted to see detailed records of research and product development, plus information about cost and availability of raw materials, transportation, warehousing and distribution, as well as sales potential.

Here Carver's unorthodox methods worked against him. The professor declared proudly that he never had reference books in his laboratory. He seldom wrote anything down, and thus had no detailed records of how his products were developed or how they performed. There was nothing a prospective investor could look at to help him understand what he was investing in. It was only natural for businessmen to expect a research lab to generate a healthy stack of experiment results, processes that failed, were modified, and then succeeded. There should be a paper trail marking the scientific quest for a marketable product, and evidence that the end result was thoroughly tested and proven. Carver literally had almost nothing.

What little he did write down gave businessmen scant comfort. When visitors questioned his notes or his results, Carver became indignant. For example, he had described a paint formula as a "sextuple oxide," which, under universally accepted chemistry terms, does not exist. Carver later claimed it was actually his description of the chemical process used to make the compound, and not the compound itself: "I call it sextuple oxide because after three years of work I am able to produce this beautiful blue only by oxidizing it six times . . . After we protect our formulas, I will be glad to show them everything I know about it."[1]

Ernest Thompson scheduled meetings in Atlanta for Carver to present his ideas to businessmen there. Thompson arranged for the professor to travel in a private railroad car as the guest of the Atlanta and West Point Railway, which would also provide his hotel accommodations. This was the sort of special attention Carver adored; it also smoothed over the many problems inherent in a black man—even a famous one—traveling to a city where he would have to ride in a segregated railroad car and would be refused entry to any upper-class hotel or restaurant.

Carver and Thompson found an eager audience in Atlanta

and soon issued a prospectus for the Carver Products Company with a capitalization of $125,000. Carver likely planned to invest some of his own savings and was slated to receive 10 percent of the net income, with a portion of his percentage going to Tuskegee. The company set up operations in downtown Atlanta and planned to open a paint factory in Chechaw. In September 1925, Carver issued a statement saying he had "practically retired from the nominal work of the Institute and will devote the remainder of my life trying to get these industries going and leave them for the benefit of our race especially, I hope."[2]

Carver seemed to have early success with an order to paint Coca-Cola barrels, but for some reason the contract was never issued. Carver filed three patents over the next two years: one for a formula and manufacturing process for cosmetics; another for pigments derived from clay and iron; and the third for other paint and stain pigments. These were the only patents Carver ever applied for in his life, and none of them ever produced a marketable product. The company never received its anticipated initial capital investment. Thompson and Carver discovered that other patents similar to theirs protected competitive products that were already well established. They also learned that the cost of a steady supply of peanut oil and meal would be high. Peanut oil was plentiful, but the presses that produced it were relatively expensive because peanut meats were so hard and required high pressure to squeeze out their oil.

By the time the Carver Products Company faded away to nothing in 1927, Carver and Thompson had found modest success with another partnership formed to make and market over-the-counter medicine. Wood creosote, a light yellow liquid extracted from the creosote bush, beech trees, and other plants, was traditionally used to treat coughing and respiratory problems. (This is a completely different compound from tar-based creosote used as a wood preservative.) Professor Carver developed a combination of creosote and peanut oil he called Penol, which he claimed made creosote taste better and work more effectively. Carver proposed Penol as a treatment for tuberculosis and began mentioning it in his speeches and interviews. Ernest Thompson, along with some other Tuskegee investors, incorporated the Carver Penol Company and launched their product in the summer of 1926. A company pamphlet assured patients that Penol was "composed of some of the best known and most proven remedies for Coughs, Sore Throat, Bronchitis, Catarrh, Pulmonary and Stomach Troubles" and was also a "Tissue Builder, Intestinal Cleanser, Germ Arrester, Nerve Food and Intestinal Antiseptic."[3]

Volume remained low and the company never made a profit. In 1929, after consumers began complaining about the quality of Penol, Thompson sold the manufacturing right to a company in Virginia for a hundred dollars a month plus a royalty of two and a half cents per bottle. The monthly fee dropped to fifty dollars and was eliminated in 1937. That year the Food and Drug Administration called Penol's claims into question; soon after, creosote was discredited as a pulmonary treatment. Not long after that, Penol disappeared from the market completely.

During the years that his prospects for commercial success declined, Carver steadily raised his profile as a speaker, scientist, and symbol of black achievement. In 1923 the professor was invited by the Commission on Interracial Cooperation to address a Southern regional meeting of the YMCA at Blue Ridge, North Carolina. Will B. Alexander, a member of the CIC, had heard the professor speak before and believed his warm, personable style would promote racial harmony in the South. Robert Russa Moton, Booker T. Washington's successor at Tuskegee, had spoken to the group in 1920 and was well received even though he ate and slept in segregated areas, away from the white participants.

Arriving at Blue Ridge, Carver was pleasantly surprised to realize that he knew the camp director, Willis D. Rutherford, from the time they had been YMCA summer delegates thirty years before. Weatherford was embarrassed and angry that Carver had to eat and sleep in segregated quarters, but feared his presence in the dormitory or dining hall would predispose his audience of white Southern boys against him. Carver told him not to worry about it.

Professor Carver was there to encourage better race relations, yet he never mentioned the topic in his speech. He talked passionately about God's miracles found in nature, and how he had provided so many wonderful creations there for the benefit of mankind. He showed the boys samples of what he had made from peanuts, sweet potatoes, and Alabama clay, demonstrating what anyone could learn about the Creator's bounty and produce using only the most basic tools and resources.

Carver held his audience spellbound. When he finished, there was a beat of absolute silence, then a roar of applause. The audience surged forward to shake his hand and speak to him. Whatever fear Willis Rutherford still had that the speech would be a failure evaporated in an instant. Several boys invited the professor to their campuses. A few weeks later Carver returned to the region to speak on six college campuses in seven days. One student newspaper reported:

> He is probably the one colored man out of a million who could have held the attention of the Clemson boys . . . To see a man as black as Doctor Carver and yet as able as he is, comes as a distinct shock to Southern boys, and jars them out of their conviction of the Negro's absolute inferiority.[4]

The next year Carver returned to Blue Ridge, sharing a cottage with students from Lynchburg College at their invitation, though he still avoided the dining hall. His hosts delivered his meals to his room. Hearing that a Negro would speak to them, delegations from Florida and Louisiana threatened to walk out. But once again Carver's engaging presence held his audience captive. No one left, and after Carver finished, the leader of the Florida delegation stood to admit what they had planned to do, and offered Carver an apology.

Two summers at Blue Ridge produced a new wave of what Carver called "my boys," correspondents he wrote to, encouraging them and nurturing their belief in the relationship between Christianity and natural science. Like the Tuskegee students he singled out for special attention, these were young men he saw as especially bright and filled with potential. They returned the admiration, grateful for the attention and guidance from someone so well known. One of Carver's young white friends later wrote of him in an article for *World Tomorrow* magazine, published in New York by the Christian pacifist Fellowship of Reconciliation:

> The man who has been and is to this day the greatest inspiration in my life is a Negro.
>
> In the whole life of this saintly man I see the future of a great race. In his eyes I see the soul of a people who experienced God and understand the meaning of the Cross.
>
> The unique contribution . . . George Carver has made in the field of science and religion is symbolical of the contribution the Negro race is destined to make to our civilization as all unequal relationships are abolished and the Negro is given every opportunity fully to develop his personality.[5]

Carver in turn credited all his admirable characteristics and accomplishments to God: the discoveries he announced were there for anyone who would study the Creator's work. In a letter written March 9, 1928, to a student named Jimmy Hardwick, the professor reiterated his point: "O if you could right now step into 'God's little Work Shop' and see what he has permitted me to do, and its effect upon the south, you would marvel."[6]

Also in 1928, Carver realized another long-held dream. During his career at Tuskegee, Carver had regularly reminded school leaders that he gave up the chance to earn his doctor-ate at Iowa State to join the faculty there. After winning the Spingarn Medal in 1923, the professor started dropping heavy hints that he would deeply appreciate an honorary doctorate. Though Iowa did not make the offer, Simpson College, where Carver had started his undergraduate career, gladly bestowed the honor. This action legitimized the "Doctor Carver" title many people used to address him already. Furthermore, it solved the problem of how a white Southerner should address him. Many whites recoiled at the thought of calling a black man "Mr." Carver. "Doctor" Carver was far more socially acceptable.

Both publicly and privately, Carver never missed an opportunity to give glory to God for his accomplishments. Though he joined church congregations at various times in his life, Carver seems not to have been the least concerned with denominational details and eagerly discussed his beliefs with people of every religious stripe. An admirer and important benefactor of Carver and Tuskegee, John D. Rockefeller, was a staunch Baptist. Other supporters ran the gamut from Baha'i to Rosicrucian. Supporters of Hindu leader Mahatma Gandhi in India wrote and visited Carver. Gandhi was leading nonviolent protests against British rule with tactics that included hunger strikes. One of his followers came to Carver at Tuskegee for recommendations on a diet for the frail vegetarian to restore his strength between fasts. Gandhi also requested copies of Carver's agricultural bulletins and sent a personal note of thanks to the professor in return. Carver answered the letter, promising to pray for him "in the marvelous work you are doing." From then on, the professor often mentioned this exchange of letters in his speeches.

Along with his research and lecturing, Carver remained a valued consultant to the peanut industry, combining his respected public profile with genuine contributions to the companies he worked with. His most significant client was Tom Huston, whose Tom Huston Company packaged and sold Tom's Peanuts and other snack foods. Carver and Huston met at the 1924 Alabama State Fair in Montgomery. Carver was there to display results of his peanut research; Huston was looking for a way to make salt grains stick to peanuts without cooking oil. The two men became friends, and Carver consulted with the Huston Company for years afterward. In 1929 Tom offered the professor a full-time job, which included use of a newly expanded research lab. As he had all other offers to leave Tuskegee, Carver politely declined. "My work is a great publicity asset for the school and for my race," he explained. "I, with others, am clannish enough to want my people to receive full credit for my work."[7]

Though he turned down the full-time position, Carver continued consulting with Huston, delivering important results. One of his most significant contributions was helping Huston figure out how to grow the Virginia variety of peanuts the company preferred in soil that had previously supported only inferior types. Virginia peanuts grown in the Deep South were immature or rotten when harvested. Company researchers believed the problem was a fungus in those regions. The senior horticulturist at the Department of Agriculture argued that the fungus was a secondary symptom caused by something else; eradicating the fungus wouldn't help because it would immediately return unless they discovered the underlying problem.

After examining a ruined crop of peanuts in the field, Carver thought the problem was a combination of several varieties of fungus, each causing a different kind of damage. The senior researcher at Huston thought Carver was more likely to be right than the USDA. The Huston team feared that the Department of Agriculture "would boo at the situation because somebody else found out" what the problem was. "Then too," they added, "people in political jobs are not looking for hard work as a rule. If they did attempt to do something, chances are they would scare the farmer to death."[8] Huston printed five thousand copies of a pamphlet detailing Carver's findings titled "Some Peanut Diseases."

Scientists and members of the public who saw Carver only as "the peanut man," unaware of his graduate study and published research on fungus, challenged his scientific conclusions. Huston hired a respected researcher named Charles Miller to review Carver's work. Miller came to admire Carver for his knowledge, his skill at collecting field specimens, and the fact that he could do so much with the meager facilities and small budgets he had to work with compared with other researchers.

The Department of Agriculture agreed to do its own survey and found that more than 20 percent of the crop was being lost, including Virginia peanuts, directly on account of the fungus, just as Carver had said. The Department developed treatments that dramatically reduced crop loss and boosted farmers' profits. In time the government recognized Carver as a collaborator, inviting him to send them plant specimens and granting him free postal privileges for them.

Tom Huston, whose job offer Carver already declined, gave the professor a cash award, which he also politely refused. To thank him for his service and saving the company many thousands of dollars in improved crop yield, Huston bought him a few gifts he thought the elderly scientist would enjoy: a typewriter, a blanket, and, as a memento, a small gold peanut. Knowing Carver had no interest in material goods but loved praise and attention, Huston commissioned a medal in his honor. Carver's likeness was sculpted in clay and cast in Italy as a bronze bas-relief. The image shows the professor writing at a table, a rack of test tubes in the background, and his lapel decorated with a sprig of cedar. There were two copies: one for the Huston laboratory and the other for Tuskegee.

Carver was beside himself with excitement—this was exactly the kind of recognition that meant so much to him. The Tuskegee copy was to be presented at graduation on May 28, 1931. Carver wrote practically everyone he knew inviting them to the unveiling. In a speech that day, Bob Barry, head of research at Huston and a great admirer of Carver's, reminded the school not to take for granted the great mind and great scientist working in their midst:

> You know him so well. But do you really know him? I see many young people here today. Do you, whom he can help so

much, really know him as he is? If you live beside a mountain and see it every day, it does not seem high to you; but someone who does not see it often knows that it is high.[9]

Such praise likely thrilled Carver almost as much as the medals.

10

IN THE MIDST OF PLENTY

Though in his sixties by this time, Dr. Carver traveled more than ever, speaking to lawmakers, teachers, farmers, and students, enthusiastically welcomed by white and black audiences alike. Both Tuskegee and the peanut industry saw the public relations power of Carver's appearances. Often one or the other of them would sponsor a trip if the hosting organization could not.

The professor's presentation changed little from place to place. Like a well-rehearsed stump speech, Carver's remarks were practiced and perfected to cover his points efficiently using his own brand of scientific proof. He spoke about the cornucopia of products derived from peanuts and the many advantages of planting them, and about the important work under way at Tuskegee educating a generation of black Americans to be self-sufficient citizens. And he never failed to give credit to the Creator who made all things, then gave his people the wisdom and energy to discover how to use them.

Carver's high-pitched voice was articulate but soft, so that his audiences had to concentrate in silence to hear him. Reporters and audience members often remarked at how the old gentleman held his listeners spellbound. One of Carver's favorite stories, and one of his most popular and often quoted, was his conversation with the Creator about the peanut. The professor added various embellishments with repeated tellings, but the versions all start with Carver asking God for knowledge about all creation. God said no. Then the professor asked the Creator to know all about just the peanut.

"All about the peanut is infinite, and you are finite," God answered. "I'd be glad to give you a few peanuts. I've given you a few brains. Take the peanuts into the laboratory and pull them into pieces."

"Can I make milk out of peanuts?" Carver inquired.

"Do you have the constituents of milk?" God asked in return.

Here during his talks, Carver would reach down behind the lectern and lift out a bottle of peanut milk. Then he revealed another peanut product, and another, often a dozen or more, to gasps of delight and rousing applause.[1]

Traveling remained a problem, however, because of his race. From a twenty-first-century viewpoint it seems a baffling and heartbreaking situation. A white couple raised Carver. He went to white churches, white colleges, and many close and influential friends from his early years were white. Yet he nor any other Negro could take an overnight train from place to place without risking an incident.

As the professor got older, Tuskegee sent an assistant, H. O. Abbott, to help with booking arrangements, luggage, and other travel details. Abbott had made Pullman sleeping car reservations for a trip between Oklahoma City and Dallas, but when they got to the train in Oklahoma City, the passenger agent refused to let them board the Pullman sleeper. Even though they had reservations, they had to sit up all night in a segregated coach car. Supposedly by law, railroads were to have a Pullman car for black passengers if there were blacks with reservations—"separate but equal" accommodations mandated by Oklahoma and Texas state law—but in practice, few black passengers could afford a Pullman ticket, and the railroad often refused to add a car to the train for only a handful of Negroes.

As the Oklahoma City *Black Dispatch* reported, "George Washington Carver, the latches of whose shoes few white men in Oklahoma are worthy to unlatch, must warm himself in the corner of a Jim Crow [segregated and substandard] coach and suffer."

Abbott wrote a letter of complaint to the railroad, who, to their credit, promised to investigate not only the incident with Dr. Carver, but their overall policy of segregating coaches where required by state law. The president of the Atchison, Topeka, and Santa Fe Railroad wrote Carver personally to assure him that the company would "be guided by what will best and most certainly insure our black passengers against disturbance and possible danger of violence or arrest and I believe that your knowledge of existing conditions . . . will enable you to understand how great is the problem and how hard it is to meet this situation wisely at all times."

In other words, while the situation had been regrettable, letting Negroes ride with white passengers could lead to the black passenger being attacked by angry whites or arrested for flaunting segregation laws. Carver was a revered public figure; somehow what was normal and legal made the railroad president uncomfortable in his case. Even so, there was little the company could do but apologize.

Long accustomed to such treatment, Carver accepted the apology with his usual kindness, thanking the railroad that "every courtesy possible will be extended to colored patrons." Some blacks thought Carver should sue. These people didn't understand the mind of George Washington Carver. Kindness, diligence, and humility were Carver's tools for dealing with the laws that made blacks second-class citizens. Abbott replied on the professor's behalf that Dr. Carver was more interested in "better traveling accommodations for our people, rather than any petty gains or notoriety."

A month later another black passenger in Oklahoma was barred from a Pullman car just as Carver had been. The *Black Dispatch* wondered again why Carver hadn't sued. Abbott sent the newspaper copies of the correspondence between Carver and the railroad, to which the editor remarked it meant "Carver can ride in a Pullman, but the rest of the niggers can't." When Abbott asked the railroad to clarify its policy, the company hinted that he and Carver should leave well enough alone: "The same elements that caused the enactment of the separate coach laws may easily bring pressure to bear on the railways to prevent more liberal interpretation of them."[2]

In 1931, the year Carver was honored with the medal presented by Tom Huston, the world economy was in a freefall that led to the worst economic depression in history. The Roaring Twenties had been prosperous times for much of America. The last half of the decade, stock market values rose an average of 22 percent a year. The nation was transformed by the automobile, which Henry Ford had made accessible to millions for the first time by producing the inexpensive Model T. So his own workers could afford one, Ford had paid them the unheard of wage of five dollars a day beginning in 1914, raised to six dollars a day in 1919. In the Twenties women won the right to vote, movies started talking, and the first commercial radio station went on the air. Easy credit and ever-increasing sales brought prosperity, even as they disguised the fact that supply was outstripping demand. The collapse of world markets beginning in the fall of 1929 sent the economy on a downward spiral lasting more than three years.

Farmers were in some of the worst economic shape of anyone. Even in the boom years, Carver's one-horse farmers had not prospered. Prices for goods and supplies they needed remained high, and industrial growth inflated the cost of machinery and spare parts. When the harvest was good, crops flooded the market and drove down prices; when it was bad, there wasn't enough to sell to break even. Then between 1929 and 1932, farm prices fell 53 percent. Since there was no federal insurance on bank deposits then, eleven thousand banks failed in four years and bank failure often wiped out depositors' life savings. Large landowners, pressed for cash and trying to improve productivity, accelerated the pace of replacing tenant farmers with tractors and other labor-saving machinery; tenants and sharecroppers by the thousands found themselves "tractored off the land."

Desperate financial times added to the value of Dr. Carver's work. His research was aimed at helping the poorest people improve their lives using the simplest means. He also began donating money to organizations for farm relief. Though he had never had a generous salary and never earned any profit from his commercial products, Carver had been saving money since his student days. Always frugal and living simply, he salted away considerable cash over the years. In addition to supporting farm charities, the professor gave many small cash gifts to friends, students, and complete strangers he saw needing help, as well as gifts of food and clothing. He had never forgotten how his classmates helped him when he was living in a shack and eking out a living doing their laundry.

Carver's gifts to others inspired gifts to him in return. Sometimes he accepted the presents, but other times he returned them, as with a check from his friend and former student Jimmy Hardwick. In a letter sent with the returned check, Carver wrote,

I knelt down by the bedside . . . and prayed for light and direction.

All day today I have made a survey of the destitute conditions and found that every family, both white and colored, had been helped and was receiving enough to keep the wolf from the door, and if they will work they will get along.

I said, "O God, this is your money." What shall I do with it that will bring the greatest returns for him?

The urge comes to return it and let you place it where God will direct it . . . I so thoroughly believe that this check is bread cast upon the waters and will return to you many fold.[3]

Carver's simple optimism and faith in God were an inspiration to others. He sincerely believed that frugality, patience, prayer, optimism, and hard work would carry financially strapped families—white and black—through hard times to a better day. He repeated this encouraging theme consistently in speeches, interviews, and letters, and in an article titled "Are We Starving in the Midst of Plenty? If So Why?" published in the January 1932 issue of *Peanut Journal*:

In Proverbs the thirteenth chapter and twenty-third verse, we have this statement: "Much food is in the tillage of the poor; but there is that which is destroyed for want of judgment." I doubt if this verse has ever had greater significance than at the present time.

We have become 99 percent money mad. The method of living at home modestly and within our income, laying a little by systematically for the proverbial rainy day which is sure to come, can almost be listed among the lost arts.

To illustrate—A few weeks ago I was visiting a large

city and was entertained in a very luxuriant home of the latest style of architecture furnished with every modern convenience, and Lincoln car of the latest model . . . Yet, when the subject of making a little sacrifice in giving and receiving Christmas presents in favor of the vast hordes of unemployed, they were not willing to do it and showed very conclusively by their system of reasoning why they needed presents this year more than ever before.

Last summer, we had an unusually large fruit and vegetable crop. Peaches, plums, figs, pears, etc., were often fed to the hogs . . . Anyone could get all the fruit they wanted for the asking, yet many families put up absolutely nothing for the winter. Their excuse being too poor to buy jars or cans. It had never occurred to them that peaches, apples, plums, pears, figs, cherries, etc, are delicious when properly dried [without using containers] . . .

Since 1928, welfare agencies . . . have sensed the need and have begun to study in a thoroughly scientific and systematic way the whole food problem as it relates to feeding the family, laying special stress upon food expenditures for low-income families, in order to give them the maximum amount of nourishment at the minimum cost . . .

Taking the peanut pound for pound, I know of no other farm, or garden, or field crop that contains as many digestible nutrients . . . The enterprising and resourceful housewife will be agreeably surprised how perfectly and cheaply she can feed the entire family . . . It is hoped that the billion pound peanut crop will be utilized in a way that will bring 100 percent nourishment, comfort, and joy especially to the many thousand jobless, undernourished people within our borders.[4]

In November of the same year, Carver published an article promoting "constructive thinking" as a way to lift the economic fortunes of the agrarian South. This, Carver explained, would "in all probability be the greatest beneficiary from the development of [creative minds] by reason of its vast wealth of undeveloped resources." While admitting that phrases like "Strike while the iron is hot" and "Take time by the forelock" were simplistic and overly familiar, he insisted they were true nevertheless.

Now is the psychological time for the creative mind to work out the many, many new uses for the inexhaustible deposits of our fine Southern clays; vegetable dye stuffs; mineral deposits, new and old; various and varied mineral waters; Southern fiber plants; material for paper pulp, and many, many other things too numerous to mention in an article of this kind.[5]

In the midst of want Carver saw the bounty of the Creator offered up to anyone who could see it and had the energy and willingness to apply himself.

A steady stream of visitors came to Tuskegee to meet Dr. Carver. Some had specific scientific questions, some came to invite him to speak or prod him to accept invitations already extended, but many of them only wanted to meet the most famous black man in the world. Whatever he was doing, he always stopped to greet them, and would continue his conversation with them as he resumed his work. Often he would show off something he had made: a sketch in chalk or colored pencil, a crocheted blanket, a pair of gloves. The legend and public persona of the old professor took on a life of its own. Stories were embellished or wholly fabricated. As before, Carver never overtly inflated his accomplishments—surely there was no need—but he never corrected hyperbolic accounts when they appeared. An article in *The Friend, A Religious and Literary Journal*, gilded the lily in dramatic style:

> For days and days he shut himself in his laboratory, saying little but working steadily. One day he spoke. What he said aroused the nation. "I have discovered," he said, "that out of the clays and sands which are in our hills in great abundance it is possible to make dyes such as the world has not seen since the days of the Egyptians . . ."
>
> Once more he shut himself in his laboratory. People awaited his results with considerable interest. This time his discoveries were hardly short of being miracles. The sweet potato was a real Aladdin's lamp, and Carver was Aladdin. At his magic touch what a concourse of products poured forth!
>
> "What next, Mr. Carver?" the world asked. "Just wait," he said, "and I will show you that the South had another lowly product out of which scores and scores of worthwhile articles can be developed to take the place of the cotton which the boll weevil is destroying." He went back to his laboratory . . . This time he took a few peanuts, the food we give to elephants

and monkeys at the circus. Lo! At his magic touch the peanut was changed into products which men never dreamed could be developed.[6]

By now Carver's list of peanut products ran to 265, with 118 for sweet potatoes and 85 for another plentiful Southern crop: pecans. As in the past, most of them were commercially impractical or uncompetitive. Nevertheless, the variety of the ideas and Carver's unflagging energy, imagination, optimism, and enthusiasm were inspiring to a nation battered by years of economic crisis and the specter of despair.

11

THE PUBLIC FIGURE

Tuskegee weathered the Great Depression better than many schools and institutions. Its facilities and resources were already modest, its students already poor, so that the worldwide economic collapse had relatively little effect. The institute celebrated its fiftieth anniversary in 1931 as the world economy plunged still lower. That year more than 2,250 students were enrolled, the second-highest number in the school's history, and the paid endowment held steady at more than 7.7 million dollars.

In 1927, Tuskegee instituted the most wide-reaching change in its history when it added college classes. Up to that time it had been strictly a "normal and industrial" center, somewhat similar to a modern community college, dedicated to giving students practical skills in order to earn a living and make their way in the world. Booker T. Washington had unwaveringly opposed any discussion of Tuskegee as a college. He considered the notion counter to his goals as well as those of the school's founders. Washington believed that blacks needed a viable trade, not lessons in Latin or ancient history. Trustees added college courses originally in order to train black teachers, but other courses soon followed. By the time of Tuskegee's fiftieth year there were more than five hundred pupils taking college subjects.

Throughout the 1930s some of the strict rules Washington insisted upon were modified or phased out. Uniform requirements were gradually relaxed and other previously ironclad rules changed or abolished. Mandatory vespers were cut from five times a week to one, yet Dr. Carver's Sunday school class remained as popular as ever. Even though he hadn't taught in the classroom for years and spent increasingly more time away from campus, students still clamored for a seat every week, filling the room to overflowing and standing along the walls.

When he wasn't on the road, Carver still lived in two rooms of Rockefeller Hall, the men's dormitory. One room was his bedroom and the other was what he called his "little den," a combination sitting room, library, art gallery, and museum. Books and magazines were stacked to the ceiling. A large glass case on one wall contained expertly sewn embroidery, tatting, and crocheting the professor had made himself. In the center of the room, a big table was covered with rock samples and stalactites. Outside each window, window boxes groaned to overflowing with flowers and other plants.

Carver remained a man of simple tastes and regular habits even as his fame grew. He got up before dawn to gather plant specimens in the woods, collecting whatever caught his eye on a particular day. After breakfast he often spent time praying that God would show him new wonders as he worked. One prayer he wrote down was, "Open thou mine eyes that I may behold wondrous things out of thy law. My help cometh from the Lord who made heaven and earth, and all that in them is." By 9:00 a.m. he was in his laboratory conducting research, meeting with an endless stream of visitors, answering letters from around the world, and visiting with students who dropped by throughout the day. After dinner he returned to his little den to read, sketch, or do needlework, and was in bed by nine.

Carver added further to the lists of products derived from peanuts, sweet potatoes, and pecans, then branched out into other crops. He experimented with making paper from wheat, matting and rope from okra, and commercial starch from artichokes. All the while his media image grew, achieving a sort of mythical status as stories about his childhood were embellished, then imprinted on the public consciousness. He was the orphan child "traded for a three-hundred-dollar horse," since his foster father, Moses Carver, had given a horse worth that much to his rescuer.

One colorful and often-quoted description of Dr. Carver came from the October 1932 issue of the *American Magazine* and was reprinted in *Reader's Digest*. James Saxon Childers visted the professor at Tuskegee and wrote a sympathetic feature article about the gentle old scientist who was guided by God as he discovered the wonders of creation for the benefit of mankind. His first impression of Carver painted an indelible picture, and remains one of the best of many similar descriptions.

The stooped old Negro shuffled along through the dust of an Alabama road at a curiously rapid rate. He was carrying an armful of sticks and wild flowers.

The sticks I could understand—he would use them for kindling—but I had never before seen an old black man ambling along the road at nine o'clock in the morning with swamp roses, wild geranium, and creeping buttercups mingled with a lot of dry sticks.

When I got a little closer to him I saw that he was wearing a saggy coat which originally might have been a green alpaca, but which the sun had faded until I couldn't be sure about the color; there were so many patches that I couldn't even be certain about the material.

The old man was walking towards a large brick building, one of the buildings of Tuskegee Institute, the famous school for Negroes at Tuskegee, Ala. His thin body bent by the years, his hair white beneath a ragged cap, he seemed pathetically lost on the campus of a great modern educational institution. Poor old fellow; I had seen hundreds just like him. Totally ignorant, unable even to read and write, they shamble along through the dust of Southern roads in search of any little odd job that will earn enough food to keep them alive, enough clothes to cover their tired old bones.

At the entrance of the building toward which we were

both walking, the old Negro turned in. "He's probably the janitor," I told myself, "and I'm sincerely glad that they've given him a job of some kind."

I stepped into the hallway. I saw a trim little secretary hurry toward the bent old Negro. I heard her say to him, "That delegation from Washington is waiting for you, Doctor Carver."[1]

The professor's public profile reached a new high with the news in 1933 that one of his peanut oil mixtures could "evidently" cure polio. Medical researchers had identified the polio virus in 1908 but had so far found no effective treatment against it. In an ironic turn, polio seemed most common in relatively clean areas. This was because the virus was widespread in dirty environments, so that people there often caught mild cases that showed no symptoms but gave them immunity from a more serious attack. The United States, sanitary by world standards, had a large number of victims, many of them children. Though most of them recovered completely, about 10 percent had limbs that were permanently weakened or deformed, or lungs damaged so badly they had to rely on mechanical breathing machines for the rest of their lives. Once a person began showing symptoms, there was nothing doctors could do to reverse or halt the damage.

Polio was newsworthy also because the president of the United States, Franklin D. Roosevelt, elected in 1932, had polio eleven years earlier at the age of thirty-nine. He walked only with great difficulty, using heavy steel leg braces, and usually made his way around the White House by wheelchair. Though he seldom mentioned the disease (and mostly kept his braces and wheelchair out of photographs), his condition naturally gave it a high profile.

The flurry of stories about Carver and polio treatment began when Carver treated an eleven-year-old boy named Foy Thompson, son of a prominent Tuskegee family. Foy was weak and underweight, and his parents thought Carver's therapeutic massage technique might help him. Locally the professor was well known as an excellent masseur. He had honed his skill as a trainer for the Iowa State football team and often gave massages to treat insomnia, poor appetite, and a host of other problems. He also used ointments that he specially mixed for various applications. Carver began treating Foy with what he called "muscle building" peanut oil massages. In a month Foy gained thirty-one pounds.

Carver's explanation was that the protein-building components in the peanut oil had been absorbed through Foy's skin into his muscles and made them bigger. The professor thought the oil and massages should have the same effect on polio patients, and began saying as much in his speeches. When a reporter asked if he had a treatment for polio, Carver replied by telegram, "Do not want any further publicity at this time. Am making more demonstrations of its efficacy."[2]

An Associated Press reporter came to Tuskegee in late 1933 for more details. The professor insisted, "It has been given out that I have found a cure. I have not, but it looks hopeful." The reporter, T. M. Davenport, used the quotation to open his story, but then went on to write at length about how close Carver might be to a cure. Of the various compounds Dr. Carver had tried to treat polio, he thought the most promising was the mixture used on Foy Thompson, which was derived from an earlier beauty-oil base he developed that seemed to build body mass. "I gave it to some ladies to use," Davenport quoted Carver as saying, "and those inclined to be fat brought it back to me [because they gained weight after using it]."

Carver told Davenport that he had treated 250 polio patients and that his peanut-based massage oil yielded the most promising results of all the formulas he tried. However, the printed quote read, "I have used it on 250 persons, and it has never failed, so far as I can find out." This sounded as if the professor had cured 250 people of polio.

From the moment Davenport's article was published on December 30, 1933, Carver was swamped with pleas for help from victims of polio, leprosy, multiple sclerosis, baldness, fallen arches, and a long list of other diseases and maladies. There was such a nationwide run on peanut oil that Carver could scarcely find enough for his own research. He insisted repeatedly that his oil and massage treatment was to help restore damaged limbs, and not a cure for polio or any other disease.

The medical community was interested in Carver's work, yet the professor's proudly unorthodox approach to science meant that he had no detailed notes, no accurate records of treatments and results, no repeatable protocol. The closer doctors questioned him, the more vague his explanations became. Carver did explain his process in more detail to a handful of friends who were doctors. He said he began his massages only after the disease had run its course and any necessary corrective surgery was complete. He had nine different versions of his formula, and spent the first week testing which one was absorbed most quickly into a particular patient's skin.

Carver instructed, "Five or six drops only of this oil should be used at a time, massaged in until every trace of it has disappeared. Repeat this as long as the skin and weak muscles will take it up, then stop until the next day. Treatment should alternate nine days of oil massage with nine days of massage without oil."

Whatever progress Carver may have made according to his own rules of scientific inquiry, the professor had incredible, undeniable success with a patient named Emmett Cox Jr., who had been crippled by polio at age two and was now a young adult. After four operations, he could walk only when wearing heavy braces on both legs from ankle to waist, and then only slowly for short distances. He started Carver's treatments in September 1934 and in six months could walk without braces.

Reader's Digest agreed to publish a feature on Cox and Carver's treatment if the medical community would endorse it. Despite a long exchange of letters and visits, no medical authority would stake its reputation on Carver's work and the story never appeared. Instead, the *Digest* reran James Saxon Childers's 1932 essay, which skirted the subject of polio treatment. Other publications picked up the story, however, and ran it with new pictures of polio patients, sparking another wave of letters and inquiries.

In 1939 President Roosevelt visited Dr. Carver at Tuskegee, where the professor gave the president a bottle of peanut oil to treat his own weak legs. A week later Carver received a letter of thanks from Roosevelt that said in part, "I do use peanut oil from time to time and I am sure that it helps."[3]

Since Carver kept no research records, there is no way to know details of his research or product trials. There is nothing in peanut oil that could restore muscles damaged by polio. There are a few documented cases of undeniable success, however, most remarkable of which was Emmett Cox. A characteristic of the disease is that in some cases, victims continue to improve slowly on their own for years after the virus has gone. Yet for Cox, Carver's treatments restored his legs. This result is likely on account of expert massage techniques that happened to improve circulation uniquely in this case, plus the professor's unwavering encouragement and enthusiasm.

THE GIFT OF HOPE

All his life, people who met George Washington Carver described him as slight, frail, small, and otherwise physically delicate. He was born prematurely, had serious respiratory problems as a child, and was never strong enough for the labor a boy or young man was expected to do. Even so, Carver had seldom been too ill to work and entered his seventies in excellent health. Rather than slowing down as he aged, Carver seemed to go faster, as devoted as ever to his research and crisscrossing the country on speaking tours.

Finally, toward the end of the 1930s, Carver began to pace himself. He traveled less, made fewer speeches, and spent less time on prospective commercial projects. He allowed his name to be used on one line of beauty products, Carvoline, but was not directly involved in developing any formulas. Rather than spending days or weeks on a speaking tour, he would go to New York or Chicago to appear on nationwide radio broadcasts, reaching a larger audience in one night than he could have expected during a long and exhausting tour.

Professor Carver also began to think more about his legacy, about preserving his work and ensuring it would continue after his death. It worried him to think that his many ongoing agricultural experiments might be abandoned once he was no longer there to oversee them. Yet at the same time, he knew himself well enough to realize that wrapping up his life's work neatly at the end of his career was not something he was likely to do. "I am not a finisher," he admitted, "I am a blazer of trails."[1]

By 1938 Carver had grown noticeably slower and weaker. He suffered bouts of anemia, took vitamin B12 shots, and spent weeks at a time in the hospital. He moved from Rockefeller Hall to Dorothy Hall, the Tuskegee guesthouse. The school started planning a museum to honor Carver, to be converted from the old laundry building next door to his new rooms. Frederick Douglass Patterson, Tuskegee's third president, had succeeded President Moton in 1935. Patterson well realized Carver's publicity value and believed a museum would not only honor a great teacher, scientist, and humanitarian but bring attention and donations to the school as well.

True to form, Carver envisioned a grand facility that told a complete and detailed story of his life. He was frustrated by delays due to lack of money and disagreements over what should be on display. The professor expected his laboratory equipment, large and ever-growing specimen collection, and paintings to be there, plus a new working research lab on the premises for his exclusive use. However, the old laundry, built in 1915, had a leaky roof requiring expensive repairs. There wasn't enough money for display cases. Carver suspected some of the faculty wanted to see the project fail. There was probably at least a grain of truth to that notion. Some of the teachers hired after Carver's retirement, as well as some students, thought Carver was a strange, somewhat demanding and fussy old man. Unaware of his national reputation, unfamiliar with him since he spent little time now with students, they mocked him behind his back and considered him self-centered. Carver probably never knew about these local critics; if he had, he would surely have said something about them.

The professor held out for a while in favor of his relatively grand museum plan, but eventually settled for a more modest display, though it still housed laboratory equipment, plants, and paintings going all the way back to his student years. The George Washington Carver Museum opened July 25, 1939, with more than two thousand guests attending the dedication.

For all his notoriety as a beloved public figure, Professor Carver remained a second-class American, subject at a moment's notice to the legal racial discrimination that endured as a legacy of Reconstruction. In September, six weeks after his gala museum opening, Carver and an assistant named Austin Curtis took the train to New York, where the professor had been invited to appear on the radio program *Strange as it Seems*. The show was based on a popular syndicated comic strip featuring bizarre or unusual stories similar to its rival, *Ripley's Believe It or Not*.

When Carver and Curtis arrived at the New Yorker Hotel,

an elegant art deco high-rise on 34th Street where Curtis had made reservations, the registration clerk eyed the pair and told them there was no vacancy. When Curtis refused to leave, the clerk offered Carver a chair in the hallway to the men's restroom where he could wait "in case any other guests checked out." The professor, nearing eighty and weary after a day and a night on the train, sat quietly while Curtis called a contact at the publisher Doubleday, Doran and Company, which was preparing a biography of Carver. A Doubleday employee came to the hotel to ask for a room, and when he got one immediately he insisted Carver and Curtis have it instead. At that, the hotel manager explained there had been a mistake and there weren't any rooms available after all. Only after a vice president of Doubleday called the New Yorker and threatened to sue was Dr. George Washington Carver, friend of President Roosevelt and Fellow of the Royal Society, shown to his room following six hours of sitting in a chair in the washroom hallway.

The accolades continued. In 1939 Carver was awarded one of three Roosevelt Medals given that year by the Theodore Roosevelt Association to honor accomplishments in fields reflecting TR's work and interests. Charles Lindbergh had received the award in 1928; one of the other 1939 honorees along with Carver was poet Carl Sandburg. Carver also accepted honorary memberships in the American Inventors Society, the Mark Twain Society, and the National Technical Society. Even Hollywood came calling. Metro-Goldwyn-Mayer, the film powerhouse that would distribute *Gone with the Wind* at the end of the year, contacted Carver about a film biography of his life and career. Carver was delighted with the idea at first, not only for the attention but also for an expected payment that would help fund the Carver Creative Research Laboratory he was trying to launch. Once he learned he would receive only a five-hundred-dollar honorarium for the project, he declined and MGM soon dropped the idea.

Late in his life, Professor Carver developed a close friendship with industrialist and inventor Henry Ford, one of the wealthiest and most prominent businessmen in America. Ford's gigantic River Rouge Plant near Detroit was a model of modern scale and efficiency that turned out cars by the tens of thousands. As a self-made man and a life-long tinkerer, Ford genuinely admired Carver's ability. Early in his career Ford built a car by hand that ended up too big to drive through the door of his workshop; he solved the problem by bashing out the brick wall on either side of the doorway with a sledgehammer. In the late 1930s Carver visited Ford at Fair Lane, his magnificent estate in the Detroit suburb of Dearborn. In time, his host built a private guest cabin for the professor at Greenfield Village, a nearby collection of historic buildings Ford had bought, moved, and refurbished (including, for example, the Wright Brothers' bicycle shop where they designed the world's first airplane) as a living history of America's industrial and cultural development.

Ford regularly stopped by Tuskegee on his way to and from Richmond Hill, his palatial eighty-thousand-acre vacation estate in Georgia, built on the site of an antebellum rice plantation. Ford constructed a school for plantation families and named it the George Washington Carver School. He invited Carver to attend the dedication and personally escorted him throughout the day's festivities. He also set up a nutritional laboratory in Carver's honor, and paid for an elevator in Dorothy Hall so Carver would have an easier time getting to and from his rooms.

≈

The old professor went to the hospital for increasingly long stays. When he was a boy, a doctor had told him he shouldn't expect to live to be twenty-one, yet here he was, still working and planning for the future at age eighty, though he walked now only with difficulty and spent much of his time in a wheelchair.

As his physical infirmities progressed, Professor Carver focused more intently than ever on his historical legacy. Three projects in particular held his attention, designed to perpetuate his memory and continue his scientific work. The first was the George Washington Carver Foundation, founded to carry on his research. Carver established it February 10, 1940, endowing it with his life savings of $32,374.19 (equivalent to half a million dollars today), a remarkable sum for someone whose income had always been so modest.

Carver's second order of business was expanding the Carver Museum into the institution he thought it should be and thought he deserved. He repeatedly asked for a larger exhibit area to display more of his paintings. Many who knew him as a scientist and teacher had no idea he was such an accomplished artist. Carver wanted all available pictures hung in one place.

He also wanted a working laboratory that would continue the plant research he had pursued for so many years.

The Tuskegee administration explained to Dr. Carver that they sympathized with his wishes but didn't have the money to fund the expansion he wanted. Carver believed the school was dragging its feet, and worried that he would die before the museum fulfilled his vision. In frustration he threatened to donate his paintings to the Alabama state archives in Montgomery. The thought of losing the pictures spurred the school to act. They found the money after all, and within a year the George Washington Carver Museum was expanded to hold seventy-one of his paintings, the largest number ever collected in one place. Henry Ford dedicated the new facilities on November 17, 1941.

An account of the opening ceremonies reflects the universal love and respect Carver enjoyed:

> There were ladies in furs, student chefs in tall white cook caps; carp[enters] with hammer heads sticking from the long pockets of their brown coveralls; student architects with rolls of drawings; white school children and grown ups; farm boys in blue overalls, nurses in uniform, a washer-woman, a dressmaker, the wife of a state senator, a telephone operator, a cotton warehouseman; colored people and white people.[2]

The third project Carver took on as a way to preserve his legacy was a biography, to be published by Doubleday, Doran and Company. The manuscript was written by Rackham Holt, the penname of Margaret Van Vechten Saunders Holt, a book critic, editor, biographer, and ghostwriter whose husband, Guy, was from a distinguished New England family. In another expression of Carver's visibility and renown, Doubleday had agreed to produce the book even before Mrs. Holt started her work. She visited Carver at Tuskegee several times and corresponded with him often. The first draft was finished by the summer of 1940, but after two years of refining and expanding, the work was still unfinished. Carver was delighted with the book because it portrayed him exactly as he wanted to be remembered: always brilliant and chronically underappreciated, "a humble genius, often maligned but never bitter, virtually flawless in every way."[3]

This was another project Carver feared would be unfinished at his death. On October 14, 1942, he wrote to Holt, as he had previously, prodding her to finish the revisions and get the book to press as soon as possible. "May I urge you again to please finish the book as I would like to have it come out while I am still able to see it."[4]

In June 1942 Carver went to visit Henry Ford in Dearborn and tour his company's research and engineering labs. The two were inseparable during their time together, with the gaunt industrialist, nearing eighty himself, showing his famous friend around day after day. Newspapers nationwide ran a photo of the white-haired old professor serving Ford a weed salad.

Decades earlier, Thomas Edison had offered Carver a job at an enormous salary. Edison and Ford had been best friends

(Edison had died at eighty-four in 1931), and during this visit Henry Ford reportedly offered Carver a job with short hours and generous terms in his experimental lab. But, despite the fact that Carver stayed with Ford until December, which added fuel to the rumors, no job offer was made public. Just before the New Year, Professor Carver came home to Tuskegee.

The trip to Michigan was to be his last. A few days after returning, Carver slipped and fell on a patch of ice when he was opening the door to his museum. He stayed in bed for two days or so and seemed to be improving. Yet he remained in pain. He never fully recovered from the fall. A few days into the New Year he drifted off to sleep and never woke up. Professor Carver died at 7:30 p.m. on January 5, 1943.

The *New York Times* led its obituary section the next day with the headline, "Dr. Carver Is Dead; Negro Scientist," and a photo of Carver. The notice touched on his work with peanuts, his remarkable childhood, and his long list of accolades and honors. It made special mention of the faith that had guided and comforted him for so long:

> A less known side of Professor Carver's activity was his Bible class at Tuskegee, started in 1906, when his office boy and seven other students asked him to teach them the Bible on Sundays. He taught the Bible by impersonating the characters himself. On one occasion he astonished his class when it reached the story of the manna-fed Israelites by producing a variety of the original manna, which he had gathered in the woods about Tuskegee.[5]

At Carver's funeral three days later in the campus chapel, Reverend C. W. Kelley read condolences and wishes from around the world. The professor was buried near Booker T. Washington. For all the tension in their relationship over the years, the two had always respected each other and always worked for the common good of black people everywhere. Forever connected in the public mind, they now rested only a short distance apart.

Professor Carver left his entire estate to his foundation. Combined with his founding gift, it totaled more than sixty thousand dollars, equal to nearly his total earnings in forty-six years at Tuskegee and valued at about a million dollars today.

Of all the praise and honor lavished on his memory, perhaps the most appropriate, and the one Carver would have appreciated most, came in a letter written by a visitor years before who had come for polio treatments.

> Upon leaving your office I remarked to my wife that I could well conceive the fact that Jesus was a man of color after knowing you. Your spirit of deep humility moved me and has made me resolve to be a better man and to attempt to live more accurately the teachings and principles of the lowly Nazarene.[6]

Professor Carver was an expert mycologist and a gifted painter, a stalwart Christian, and an inspiring teacher. Yet the world knew him as the Peanut Man, even though his work on peanuts, while vast and impressive, had little scientific documentation and produced no commercial successes. Of all his accomplishments, it may be that his greatest gift to black people and to the world was the gift of hope. He proved that a black man—or any man—could start with nothing and achieve great things. He encouraged farmers and gave them practical advice for scratching out a living when encouragement was in short supply and living was hard. Carver believed that the way to overcome prejudice and discrimination was not by complaining, but by proving that the notion of black inequality was a myth born of ignorance. He was convinced that the Creator made great things to be discovered, and gave him the passion and the ability to discover them.

EPILOGUE

George Washington Carver is largely forgotten today, displaced as a symbol of black achievement by men and women invested more in high-profile confrontation than in the patient, incremental progress Carver represented. His gentle ways and passive personality were swamped by the racial upheavals of the 1960s. Since that time, he has remained largely a marginal figure in American history. Even the Carver Museum, dedicated to keeping the professor's memory alive, fell on hard times. In 1947 it was heavily damaged by fire. The building itself, made of bricks molded and walls built by Tuskegee students, withstood the blaze, as did many of the scientific displays. The great tragedy was Carver's paintings. Of the seventy-one in the collection, only a handful survived, making a George Washington Carver canvas one of the most rare in the art world. The museum was rebuilt, further enlarged, and reopened in 1951.

George Washington Carver deserves a place at the table with the thinkers and doers who led America toward greatness by encouraging them to look to science for answers, to themselves for strength and resolve, and to God for guidance and assurance.

In the generations since Carver's death, the world has been transformed into a place he would scarcely recognize. Tuskegee students today enjoy a level of personal comfort and convenience unimaginable to him. The dining hall Carver worked so hard to supply under such frustrating circumstances isn't even run by students—it is catered by Marriott. Most incredible of all would be that, at this writing, the president of the United States is half African.

Still, for all the differences, some core elements of Carver's legacy stand resolutely unchanged. His commitment to training scientists at Tuskegee is alive and strong. The school of veterinary medicine there has trained 70 percent of black veterinarians in America (though some years only 20 percent of the school's enrollment is black—applicants come from around the world). After Jonas Salk developed a polio vaccine in 1953, Tuskegee provided more than six hundred thousand vaccine cultures worldwide for experimentation and testing, fulfilling Carver's dream of defeating this terrible disease. And Dr. Carver's agricultural experiment station continues strong. Student scientists, under contract to NASA, are developing ways to grow sweet potatoes in outer space to feed astronauts on their way to Mars.

Of all the experiments and programs and peanut products George Washington Carver left behind, his greatest gift is a legacy of hope: a timeless message to black and white, rich and poor, farmer and factory owner, through word and deed, that God made us all and has given us everything we need to find our sunlit place in the Creator's world.

ACKNOWLEDGMENTS

Librarians and archivists are indispensable to a biographer. I was fortunate that my research on George Washington Carver led me to the Hollis Burke Frissell Library at Tuskegee University, where Cynthia Wilson and Loretta Robinson kindly guided me through the stacks, shared their knowledge, and brought hamburgers at just the right time.

I'm especially grateful to Professor Sheridan Howard Settler, former colleague of Carver's, who walked through the rain to meet me and share his memories of teaching at Tuskegee during the years Carver's fame was approaching its peak. Thanks also to Dr. B. D. Mayberry, who recounted his experiences of studying both botany and the Bible under Dr. Carver.

Closer to home, this project has benefited from the insights and skill of my friends at Thomas Nelson: Joel Miller, Kristen Parrish, Heather Skelton, and Lisa Schmidt. Thanks as well to Janene MacIvor, whose editorial eye has improved the writing considerably from the place where it started. Once again, my friend and agent, Andrew Wolgemuth, managed to keep me on track and on time rather than veering off the road as I am wont to do occasionally.

And closest of all, I am grateful for my children, Charles

and Olivia. Though they're all grown up now (everybody warned me it would happen) they still give me a sense of perspective no one else can give, and remind me daily of the joy and promise the world has to offer if I will only see it.

NOTES

CHAPTER 1   CARVER'S GEORGE
1. Gary R. Kremer, ed., *George Washington Carver in His Own Words* (Columbia: University of Missouri Press, 1987), 23.
2. John Perry, *Unshakable Faith* (Sisters: Multnomah, 1999), 126.
3. Ibid., 128.

CHAPTER 2   WANDERING YEARS
1. Robert P. Fuller, "The Early Life of George Washington Carver," Washington DC: National Park Service, 26 November 1957.
2. Perry, 137.
3. Ibid., 139.
4. "Friends of Old Days in Kansas Saw Budding Genius of Negro Scientist," Kansas City *Star*, 9 September 1942. (Typed copy in Simpson College archives.)
5. Kremer, 45.

CHAPTER 3   THE ROAD TO TUSKEGEE
1. Kremer, 46.
2. Ibid., 47.
3. Linda O. McMurry, *George Washington Carver: Scientist and Symbol* (Oxford: Oxford University Press, 1981), 41.
4. Ibid.
5. Ibid., 46.
6. Perry, 76.
7. McMurry, 43.

CHAPTER 4   *PRESSURES AND POLITICS*
1. Kremer, 64.
2. Ibid., 67.
3. Perry, 169.
4. Ibid., 169–70.
5. McMurry, 49.
6. Ibid., 231.
7. Kremer, 70.
8. Perry, 223.
9. Kremer, 71.
10. Ibid., 73.

CHAPTER 5   *FROM POWER TO POWER*
1. McMurry, 116.
2. Perry, 238–9.
3. McMurry, 103.
4. Ibid., 104.
5. Perry, 249.
6. Ibid., 286.
7. Ibid., 252.
8. Ibid., 253.
9. Ibid.
10. Ibid., 254–6.
11. McMurry, 136.
12. Perry, 258.
13. Ibid., 259.
14. Ibid., 259–60.
15. Ibid., 260.

CHAPTER 6   *OUT OF THE SHADOW*
1. Perry, 240.
2. Ibid., 284.
3. Ibid., 286–7.
4. Ibid., 287.
5. Ibid., 288.
6. Ibid.

7. Booker T. Washington, "The Fruits of Industrial Training," *Atlantic Monthly* vol XCII (October 1903): 453–62.

8. McMurry, 157.

9. "A Plea for His Race," *Atlanta Constitution*, 19 September 1895, 1, col. 1.

10. Perry, 299.

11. McMurry, 158.

12. Perry, 305.

13. Horace D. Slatter, "Men I Have Known," *The Afro-American*, Baltimore, 14 October 1916.

CHAPTER 7   *SCIENCE SHALL MAKE YOU FREE*

1. All quotations from the hearing transcript are in Kramer, 103–13.

2. Perry, 313.

3. McMurry, 177.

4. Perry, 315.

5. Pauline A. Young, "George Washington Carver," *The Tuskegee Alumni Bulletin* 4 no. 12 (December 1922), 5ff.

6. Walter Hoff Seely, "Carver of Tuskegee," *Success* magazine, 1923.

7. Perry, 316.

CHAPTER 8   *SIMPLY THE TRUTH*

1. Kramer, 172.

2. Perry, 313.

3. Ibid., 318.

4. Ibid.

5. Ibid., 323.

6. "Form Company to Market Products of Plant Wizard," *Atlanta Constitution*, 20 September 1923.

7. Perry, 324.

8. Ibid.

9. "Men of Science Never Talk That Way," *New York Times*, 20 November 1924, 22, col. 6.

10. Kramer, 129–30.

11. Perry, 326.

CHAPTER 9   *THE PEANUT MAN*
1. McMurry, 183.
2. Ibid., 191.
3. Ibid., 192–3.
4. Ibid., 205.
5. Perry, 331.
6. Kremer, 176.
7. Perry, 335.
8. Ibid.
9. Ibid., 337.

CHAPTER 10   *IN THE MIDST OF PLENTY*
1. Perry, 337–8.
2. This entire episode is quoted from the *Oklahoma City Black Dispatch*, 13 February 1930; follow-up 14 August and 21 August 1930.
3. Kremer, 178.
4. Entire article is reprinted in Kremer, 117–19.
5. Ibid., 120.
6. Perry, 348.

CHAPTER 11   *THE PUBLIC FIGURE*
1. James Saxon Childers, "A Boy Who Was Traded for a Horse," *The American Magazine*, October 1932, 24ff.
2. McMurry, 243–7 for Carver's comments here and following about his polio treatments.
3. Ibid., 253.

CHAPTER 12   *THE GIFT OF HOPE*
1. Perry, 354.
2. Tampa *Bulletin*, 29 November 1941.
3. Perry, 357.
4. Ibid.
5. "Dr. Carver Is Dead; Negro Scientist," *New York Times*, 6 January 1943, 25, col. 1.
6. McMurry, 254–5.

BIBLIOGRAPHY

"A Plea for His Race." *Atlanta Constitution*, 19 September 1895, 1, col. 1.

Carver, George Washington. "Experiment Station Bulletin No 1: Feeding Acorns." Tuskegee: Normal School Steam Press, 1898.

Childers, James Saxon. "A Boy Who Was Traded for a Horse." *The American Magazine*, October 1932, 24ff.

"Dr. Carver Is Dead; Negro Scientist." *New York Times*, 6 January 1943, 25, col. 1.

"Form Company to Market Products of Plant Wizard." Atlanta *Constitution*, 20 September 1923.

"Friends of Old Days in Kansas Saw Budding Genius of Negro Scientist," Kansas City *Star*, 9 September 1942.

Fuller, Robert P. "The Early Life of George Washington Carver." Washington DC: National Park Service, 26 November 1957.

Harlan, Louis R. *Booker T. Washington: The Making of a Black Leader 1856–1901*. New York: Oxford University Press, 1972.

——. *Booker T. Washington: The Wizard of Tuskegee, 1901–1915*. New York: Oxford University Press, 1983.

Holt, Rackham. Galleys and notes for her biography of George Washington Carver at the library archives, Tuskegee University.

Kremer, Gary R., ed. *George Washington Carver in His Own Words*. Columbia: University of Missouri Press, 1987.

McMurry, Linda O. *George Washington Carver: Scientist and Symbol*. Oxford: Oxford University Press, 1981.

"Men of Science Never Talk That Way." *New York Times*, 20 November 1924, 22, col. 6.

Oklahoma City *Black Dispatch*, 13 February; 14 August; 21 August 1930.

Perry, John. *Unshakable Faith*. Sisters: Multnomah Publishers, 1999.

Seely, Walter Hoff. "Carver of Tuskegee." *Success* magazine, 1923.

Slatter, Horace D. "Men I Have Known." *The Afro-American*, Baltimore, 14 October 1916.

Tampa *Bulletin*, 29 November 1941.

Washington, Booker T. "The Fruits of Industrial Training." *Atlantic Monthly* vol XCII (October 1903): 453–62.

ABOUT THE AUTHOR

John Perry was born in Kentucky and grew up in Houston, Texas. He attended University College, Oxford, England, and graduated *cum laude* from Vanderbilt University in Nashville. John has appeared on C-SPAN *Book TV*, *The Janet Parshall Show*, *The G. Gordon Liddy Show*, and other syndicated programs. He has published biographies of Charles Colson, Gov. Mike Huckabee, Booker T. Washington, George Washington Carver, Mary Curtis (Mrs. Robert E.) Lee, and Sgt. York among others. His coauthored novel, *Letters to God*, is a *New York Times* Best Seller. John lives in Nashville.

Close Encounters of the Christian Kind

— Available Now —

JANE AUSTEN
9781595553027

ANNE BRADSTREET
9781595551092

WILLIAM F. BUCKLEY
9781595550651

JOHN BUNYAN
9781595553041

WINSTON CHURCHILL
9781595553065

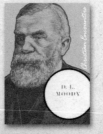

ISAAC NEWTON
9781595553034

D. L. MOODY
9781595550477

J. R. R. TOLKIEN
9781595551078

SAINT PATRICK
9781595553058

**SAINT
FRANCIS**
9781595551078

**SAINT
NICHOLAS**
9781595551153

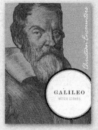

**JOHANN
SEBASTIAN BACH**
9781595551085

**SERGEANT
YORK**
9781595550255

GALILEO
9781595550316

Available August 2011

**FYODOR
DOSTOEVSKY**
9781595550347